A JOURNEY OF
DIVERSITY &
INCLUSION
IN SOUTH AFRICA

Endorsements

The South African story needs to be told from all angles. It is never one story and perfect for all time; it is a growing and developing story. Nene Molefi has done us proud. By producing this against the backdrop of her own life, her business and public service interests, as well as her faith perspective, we get a rich tapestry of freedom, faith and dedication. I wish that every South African should read this book and be inspired.

Prof Barney Pityana, Thabo Mbeki Foundation, former Principal and Vice Chancellor of the University of South Africa, Professor Emeritus of Law, University of South Africa, and Honourary Professor in Philosophy, Rhodes University

An excellent, insightful and essential guide for how we can break through barriers to transform ourselves as a society, so that we can finally discover and celebrate the strength that comes from our diversity.

S'ne Mkhize, Senior Vice President: Group Human Capital, Sasol

As a Tsonga speaking person who has had first-hand experience of the unconscious bias against the unchangeable characteristics of my being, I relate well to Nene's story and journey of self-discovery and awareness — both from my time as a young student and as a young professional. She has intelligently captured the key issues which resonate with many who grew up during that era which some choose to ignore. She manages to dive deeply into how the issues have evolved in post-Apartheid South Africa and touches a nerve where many dare not tread. Her thought-provoking recommendations force us to genuinely reassess our outlook when it comes to issues of culture, diversity and transformation. This is a well-articulated story and a book that is relevant for all South Africans.

Ntsako Baloyi, Community Development Manager, Coca Cola Beverages SA

Nene Molefi's book, *A Journey of Diversity & Inclusion in South Africa*, is a reflective story that draws on her real lived experiences as a black woman leading and facilitating transformation in South Africa. It is written in accessible, non-judgemental language, and will resonate with many people who are interested in diversity and inclusion, both in South Africa and across the globe. Nene uses herself as a tool, and her honest, critical self-reflections, as well as her Tips and Guidelines at the end of each chapter, elevate the book to be more than an autobiographical piece: it is all at once an educational text, a consulting guide, and a personal and professional developmental guide. Nene's book will help readers, young and old, and from all walks of life, to do their own critical self-reflections as they continue on their transformation journeys. This augers well for individual, familial, organisational and societal transformation in South Africa, and indeed globally.

Prof Peliwe P Mnguni, Associate Professor
(PhD Leadership and Org Dynamics), UNISA (SBL)

This book is an invaluable resource, not only for organisations but for all communities in Africa and beyond. The stories of diversity and inclusion Nene includes are rooted in our upbringing and that is where the work must begin. The messages we communicate to the children and how these get embedded in their minds and carried through to adulthood point to the ongoing collaborative work needed between academics, corporate leaders and community workers. This is an enjoyable read with great tips for all leaders.

Zanele Mbeki, Founder & Patron, WDB Trust

Nene addresses the sensitive topic of transformation in a holistic way that helps businesses to understand why prioritising this is good for all of us. The concept of connecting the head, heart and hands is a simple and yet very powerful way of ensuring that progress is made when it comes to diversity and inclusion. This topic, by its nature, is covered in a way that promotes inclusion, whilst tackling some of the challenges that corporate SA has faced in the past. The tools provided in the book will help organisations achieve meaningful changes. It's a must read for any South African who wants to understand how we can address issues of diversity and inclusion in a long lasting way.

Dr Liziwe Masoga: Human Resources Executive, Old Mutual Insure

Writing a book from your own life experiences and then putting that into practice is quite a remarkable feat. The book highlights the complexity associated with diversity and the many biases we are not always aware of. This is a very practical and easy to read book, which will be of value to any diversity facilitator. The lessons learned, practical experiences, insights, and tips will be of value to South Africans of all races, gender and age groups. By reading this book, people of all races can learn to better understand and accept one other.

Prof Nico Martins, Research Professor, Department of Industrial and Organisational Psychology at the University of South Africa, Unisa

Despite a world of 7bn inhabitants, societies are becoming less inclusive and more intolerant of difference. This contribution helps us to understand how our society, organisations and us as individuals have overt but also deeply ingrained biases, and how we as leaders can be more understanding and deliberate to overcome them. Congratulations to Nene Molefi in capturing both her personal journey and her two decades of experience working with executives teams globally on this critical topic.

Shaun Rozyn, Global Programs Leader: Saudi Arabian Basic Industries Corporation, Riyadh, Saudi, Arabia

This is an outstanding piece of work and I can sense an emotionally palpate concept of Ubuntu on each page of this book.

Having grown up in Rwanda and now working in SA, this a loud wake-up call to me about how social biases can be detrimental to society, cause harm to others, and lead to extreme inhumane practices such as apartheid, genocide and holocausts. In my medical profession I am constantly hurt by how people treat each other — carelessly putting each other down; embracing our diversity and being inclusive would cater for all layers of the profession for the betterment of our noble profession.

Thank-you Nene, for such an inspirational narrative, which I recommend to all young people, parents, educators, medical doctors and mentors who strive to make a positive difference in society.

The practical tips provided do not leave us in despair but provide hope and focus, irrespective of the surrounding circumstances. I recommend any young person and any doctor to learn from and emulate these.

Dr James Nkurunziza, MD: Physician Cardiologist, Kigali, Rwanda

Nene has boldly and authentically dealt with the real issues in the social and business communities in modern Africa and provided solutions that are fresh and doable. Her model for culture change and the 'three H' leadership concepts, together with the idea of putting 'being' before 'doing' are principles that would bring transformation of life at the personal level and the work environment in any society. Her belief in "using your rank, power, and position to positively influence an environment and make another person's life easier" is a concept that cuts across all forms of leadership and will benefit all leaders even at family level where it all begins. This book is revolutionary in practical ideas and concepts and is destined to transform lives and communities. Try it.

Dr Sam Misiani, Life Coach, Communication and Media Director. WKUC, KENYA

Nene Molefi's book, *A Journey of Diversity & Inclusion in South Africa*, is a major contribution to the field. It is part autobiography and part textbook on how to do and lead D&I work well. Nene is a compelling and consummate storyteller who writes from the heart with keen perceptions about society at large (especially South Africa). Her storytelling makes the lessons learned — set out clearly through insights and tips at the end of each chapter — a pleasure to read.

Dr Alan Richter, President QED Consulting, New York, USA

Nene shares her wisdom not just as a professional practitioner, but also by acknowledging the most important learning by sharing so vulnerably her own story. I am not sure there is any better way to share wisdom if it is not intertwined with both professional and personal experiences! She has written her pearls of wisdom while compassionately instigating the opportunity for transformation for the reader. She transcends the stories to principles that we all can take away; know your own story and be transformed only if you are willing to take ownership! I hope this book reaches everyone from the people on the ground we call grassroots to those in leadership positions we call treetops.

Dr. JuanCarlos Arauz, Founding Executive Director of E3:
Education, Excellence & Equity, USA

Unflinching, incisive and heartfelt, this book is a compelling call to action. It dissects and tackles head-on through frank discussion, practical insights and tips the challenges and questions that lie at the heart of what is required to create change, inclusivity and social cohesion in both our workplaces and our society. Nene is one of those people who inspires me and gives me faith in the new and inclusive South Africa that we can all create professionally at work and personally in our lives. If not us, then who?

Heidi Carter, Centre for Conscious Leadership

A deeply authentic personal narrative combined with powerful and practical insights from one of South Africa's foremost advisors on diversity and transformation. All too often, corporate transformation programmes run the risk of losing touch with the personal issues that impact so strongly on the lives of each employee. Nene Molefi's excellent book is a potent reminder of the impact of personal experience, both past and current, on how we all function at work and in life. It should be required reading for any leader who is serious about effectively transforming their organisation.

Dr Jonathan Broomberg, CEO, Discovery Health

Provocative, beautifully told stories lie at the core of Nene's open account of her encounters with the unacknowledged biases that lie within each of us. Nene's gift, however, goes further than her personal accounts as a child, student, employee, entrepreneur and facilitator. Her ability to rest the account of her life on a bedrock of accessible theory is masterful. So too is her extension of her narrative into practical recommendations that, if diligently pursued, will enable all of us to meaningfully interpret and articulate our own biases, narratives and the contributions we can make to heal our fractured nation.

Prof Nicola Kleyn, Dean, The University of Pretoria's Gordon Institute of Business Science (GIBS)

Nene Molefi's book is instructive on how the work of creating a transformed and inclusive society is ongoing and important for all of us. Diversity and inclusion is not only good for business, it the right thing do regardless of legislation given our long history of racial segregation and exclusion. It is no longer good enough to say "diversity is an asset". Leaders are expected to lead the way of inclusion, to live the values, and to define the DNA of their organisation in more visible ways with their head, heart and hands.

Bongani Nqwababa, Joint President & Chief Executive Officer, Sasol Limited

A Journey of Diversity & Inclusion in South Africa is mind-opening for those yet to be convinced of the need for transformation, and helpful to those who are already committed to transformation but are not sure how to play a part. The examples and references are insightful, relatable and practical because Nene draws from her personal transformation journey in South Africa, as well as her professional experiences in corporates and communities. This book will empower willing transformers.

Thulani Sibeko, Nedbank Executive for Marketing, Communications and Corporate Affairs

Knowing someone's story is a path to understanding and empathy. Reading Nene's story isn't only about knowing Nene — although that is reason enough to read her story; it is about learning of a culture and a country that merits understanding. Her book helps us broaden our awareness and enables us to dig deeply into authenticity. She offers a personal and professional model that all of us who want to make a difference in this world would benefit from by reading.

Julie O'Mara, President, The Centre for Global Inclusion, Co-author Global Diversity & Inclusion Benchmarks, Former National President, Association for Talent Development, Las Vegas, USA

Nene Molefi is a national treasure. With a deep understanding of how difference can hurt and can heal, she has written a moving and wonderful book that is touching in its humanity, universal in its wisdom and bracing in its practicality. Employing the acute observational powers and generosity of heart for which she is known, she has produced the classic guide to making diversity flourish at work and in life. With this book she teaches us that being a true South African and one's own best self are one and the same.

Stephan Malherbe, Chair, Genesis Analytics

Nene Molefi has written a must read in *A Journey of Diversity & Inclusion in South Africa*. The release of the book comes at an opportune time when our beloved country and continent is plagued with a number of challenges around what it truly means to be African.

With her extensive experience in this field of diversity and inclusion, Nene pulls together her life experiences and insights - this is a book that all leaders and HR practitioners should read and refer to on matters of diversity management.

Thank-you Nene, for a thought provoking and insightful guide that we can learn from both professionally and personally.

Tirelo Sibisi, Executive Vice President, Group Human Resources, AngloGold Ashanti

A mind-blowing miracle of our world and life is its rich diversity, also of people. Nene's book is a passionate appeal to all of us to treasure diversity like a precious vase containing expensive perfume, which, if handled with care, can make amazing things happen by unlocking the best in people. Taking the reader along on her personal life journey as an intimate case study in diversity, from an inside-out, experiential perspective, she distils front line, tested wisdom and practical tips with respect to diversity. Her shared, rich insights — so eloquently communicated — challenges, enables and empowers all of us to transform our heads, hearts and hands by uncompromisingly applying the master key of genuine inclusion to everyone regardless, in the full range of their wonderful variety.

Prof Theo Veldsman, Psychology Department, University of Johannesburg

Using her own personal journey, Nene Molefi has masterfully chronicled three decades of the struggle for inclusion in South Africa. With poignant stories and historical references, she educates the reader both from the head and the heart. No matter what part of the world you call home, if you want to understand the complexities of difference, this is a must read.

Mary-Frances Winters, President and CEO, The Winters Group, Inc.,.USA

This is a book that no leader, workplace, school or family that is committed to this country should be without. Written in an accessible, inspiring, personal and thought-provoking style, this book is one you will want to own and refer to again and again.

Karien Norval, Director, Cheadle Thomson and Haysom

First published in 2017

ISBN: 978-1-86922-703-6
eISBN: 978-1-86922-704-3 (ePDF)

Published by KR Publishing
P O Box 3954
Randburg
2125
Republic of South Africa

Tel: (011) 706-6009
Fax: (011) 706-1127
E-mail: orders@knowres.co.za
Website: www.kr.co.za

Printed and bound: HartWood Digital Printing, 243 Alexandra Avenue, Halfway House, Midrand
Typesetting, layout and design: Cia Joubert, cia@knowres.co.za
Cover design: Marlene de Villiers, marlene@knowres.co.za
Editing & proofreading: Jennifer Renton, jenniferrenton@live.co.za
Project management: Cia Joubert, cia@knowres.co.za
Index created with TExtract / www.Texyz.com

A JOURNEY OF
DIVERSITY &
INCLUSION
IN SOUTH AFRICA

GUIDELINES FOR LEADING INCLUSIVELY

BY

NENE MOLEFI

publishing

2017

Acknowledgements

To God, who is my banner, my anchor, my centre in everything I do. This book is an answered prayer; my dream project of many years.

Family Acknowledgements

TO MY BEAUTIFUL CHILDREN

Masebedi, Motheo and Tlhalefang, who have seen me navigating between parenting, owning a business, church responsibilities and writing a book.

Those morning and evening family prayer sessions have done wonders for this book project and our lives in general.

May they read this book and pick up lessons I leant from their grandmother who died before any of them were born. But because great lessons outlive the lives of those who lead them, I hope they treasure this gift.

To my cousin Johanna who has been my pillar of strength, my support system and mother to all these three children; may God bless you mightily and give you strength.

Work Acknowledgements

To Jennie Tsekwa, who was involved in the beginning chapters of this book, dreaming with me and co-shaping its structure and listening to my story when it was just a story, and working with me to put some thoughts down on paper.

To Lee Middleton, a writer who got involved in the second phase of this project, editing, guiding and most importantly keeping me focused and accountable to my own set goals and time frame. Without her strict coaching, this book would not have been realised at this time.

To Bongani Ndaba, who tirelessly read chapter by chapter of the manuscript and gave his advice and comments. He did it with so much passion that after each chapter he would make me more excited about the project, like he was injecting life into it on the days when I doubted that it was a good book to publish.

Many others also contributed to a greater or lesser extent to make this possible.

Table of Contents

About the Author

Nene Molefi, who was born in Soweto, is the CEO of Mandate Molefi HR Consultants, a company with a track record that spans over 16 years.

Her versatility and experience in partnering with boards and executive committees has positioned her well to work with large scale culture change, transformation and leadership development projects.

Over the past 18 years, Nene has gained a reputation both locally and internationally as a thought leader in diversity and inclusion, values-driven leadership and transformation. She is a regular presenter at conferences around the world, including Malaysia, Bangladesh, the USA, Zimbabwe and Zambia. She has authored numerous publications, including a chapter in *Leadership Perspectives from the Front Line*. She is an expert panelist for a Diversity & Inclusion Benchmark Tool, and is a member of the Diversity Collegium, a think tank of globally recognised diversity experts.

Nene qualified with a BSoc Work from the University of Fort Hare, a BSoc Sc from the University of Cape Town and a Masters in Leading Change and Innovation from York St John University: York, UK.

Nene has also written a chapter in the book *Organisational Diagnosis*. She is also a newly appointed board member of The Centre of Global Inclusion based in the USA, sits on the advisory structure of the Auditor General of SA and is a board member of the community Aids Response. Nene is an associate lecturer at GIBS on Global Diversity and Unconscious Bias, as well as an associate lecturer on Transformation Strategy for Stellenbosch Business School. Nene is committed to social entrepreneurship and her community. She sits on the board of Meals on Wheels, a non-profit organisation that provides food to the homeless and those in need in South Africa. Her e-mail is nene@mandatemolefi.co.za.

Social justice, fairness and inclusion are vital values, and essential practical goals, for all South Africans. This book highlights the importance of dialogue on diversity and inclusion. It comes at a defining moment for our country where change is greatly needed, and it challenges us to *think* differently — about others and ourselves. And beyond just thinking differently, this book challenges us to **be** different, to **act** differently, to **notice** how our *being* — our behaviours, biases and attitudes — impact on those around us. It invites us to listen and to observe more closely the nuances that are the key to creating a more inclusive future for all.

And this challenge is by no means limited to the South African context. The ideas and experiences shared by author Nene Molefi speak directly to the troubling prejudices and inequities that persist in our world. Diversity and inclusion are more pressing than ever. Injustices and deep social divisions persist personally and systemically. Racism, sexism, homophobia, and other forms of fear and hatred are not isolated; they remain embedded and they demand courageous, deliberate work.

And naming the problem is not enough. We need creative thinkers and actors who are committed to change; who are willing to challenge themselves and others to lead with integrity and to share their stories of success and failure.

Nene Molefi is the owner and managing director of a consulting firm that specialises in change and transformation. She is well placed to guide us. She has been working with companies, state-owned entities and government agencies for almost 20 years.

Nene always strikes me by her practical knowledge and humane insights.

She has led many transformation interventions, and she is willing to learn and adapt to our changing environment. She is the first black South African to be a member of the Diversity Collegium, a global think-tank of diversity experts, and she is a board member of the Center for Global Inclusion. She speaks at conferences around the world and she is a guest speaker and associate lecturer for some of South Africa's leading business schools.

I have had the privilege of attending one of her diversity and inclusion workshops within the judiciary; the impact was palpable. The judiciary recalled her to run another series of workshops, which has happened in the many other sectors where she has worked.

In this book, Nene uses her own story to cast a bright light on the transformation journey. In Part 1, titled 'The Early Years', she begins her story with a vivid portrait of life in Soweto from the mid-70s to the early-80s, a tumultuous time during which her mother laid a solid foundation for her, modelling the values of persistence, courage and abundance. She describes the challenge of pursuing education with limited resources and succeeding as one of the few from her Matric class to be accepted at university.

Her journey progresses from an undergraduate degree at Fort Hare, where her political insights were triggered, to an Honours degree at UCT, where she encountered the sharp edges of social difference and micro-inequities. But this did not stop her. Hers has been a life of firsts. After UCT, she became the first black social worker at the Red Cross Hospital in Cape Town. Then for several years she worked for Eskom, developing innovative interventions on HIV/AIDS and many other issues affecting employees. She deeply understands the effects of prejudice and discrimination, but she also knows the power of unofficial mentors who empower her and others.

In Part 2, titled 'Moving into Transformation Work', Nene describes her secondment to the Department of Labour, where she worked with dynamic people in formulating key labour legislation, including the Employment Equity Act. While relating what she experienced, she challenges some of the common complaints and misperceptions about that statute and its implementation. She then describes her experience as the head of transformation for the City of Cape Town, where she faced barriers that impeded her work.

Part 3, 'Taking Ownership', provides an intimate look into how Nene established her own consulting firm. Here she reckoned with the often invisible challenges faced by black and female consultants. But she also recounts the many opportunities she seized. She describes her model for culture change in very practical terms, giving examples of companies that have benefited from a more structured and systematic approach to transformation.

She concludes with two powerful chapters on what it means to truly lead, as well as doing the inner work required to be a truly transformative leader.

More than other books on leadership, Nene's book quite vulnerably takes the reader on her personal journey. In addition to the deeply personal content, each chapter ends with practically useful 'Insights and Tips'.

Nene does not present herself as an all-knowing expert. Instead, she shows the power of dealing with one's own issues to become a co-creator of change. Whatever our life specificities — race, gender, sexual orientation, age — introspection is indispensable. And we must be willing to unlearn the negative things we were taught about those different from us. Nene's book offers hope and substance in our vision of a diverse, inclusive and just society.

But she requires us to be challenged. Allow yourself to be uncomfortable and ask the difficult questions, but also be encouraged. Change is possible. It starts inside.

Friday July 14, 2017

Acronyms Used

AIDS	Acquired Immune Deficiency Syndrome
ANC	African National Congress
B-BBEE	Broad-Based Black Economic Empowerment
BCF	Black Consultative Forum
BEE	Black Economic Empowerment
CASAC	Council for the Advancement of the South African Constitution
CBD	Central Business District
DG	Director General
DoL	Department of Labour
EE	Employment Equity
Exco	Executive Committee
HIV	Human Immunodeficiency Virus
HQ	Headquarters
JSE	Johannesburg Stock Exchange
LD	Learning and Development
MBA	Master of Business Administration
OPS	Operations
SABC	South African Broadcasting Corporation
SABSWA	South African Black Social Workers Association
SGMs	Senior General Managers
UCT	University of Cape Town
UIF	Unemployment Insurance Fund

Chapter 1

UNPACKING OUR BAGGAGE

How early messages form (1965-1982)

We desire to bequeath two things to our children; the first is roots, the other is wings.

Sudanese Proverb

LIKE MOST *DIVERSITY AND INCLUSION* JOURNEYS, mine started at home. I was born in Soweto, a township in the south of Johannesburg. I grew up in that historically inclusive working class melting pot, where it was not at all strange to hear people switching between a medley of languages, from Setswana and isiZulu to Xitsonga, Sepedi and Sesotho. As kids, we unconsciously accommodated one another, speaking milder versions of our mother tongues to friends who didn't share them. In my memory, Soweto buzzed with the playful energy of children playing popular township games like Bhathi, Dibeke or Black Mampatile; running through the streets dodging cars, or over to the neighbour to 'borrow' an onion or cup of sugar. Soweto's soundtrack was the jingle of the soft-serve ice cream truck trundling down the road, and its smell that of coal burning in the stoves lit by us girls every afternoon like clockwork.

Despite sheltering a wide range of cultural diversity — including individuals drawn to the riches of Johannesburg's surrounding mines or forced to move to the city due to the migrant labour system — the Soweto of my childhood was an environment that provided little to no contact with other races. We were diverse as Africans, but due to the government's policy of apartheid, Johannesburg's coloured and Indian people lived in different neighbourhoods. White people could have been on another planet as far as I was concerned. Meanwhile, most of us Africans had not yet awakened to Steve Biko's black consciousness philosophy. Black people from other African countries were viewed with caution, curiosity or even suspicion. This, however, did not include those from Botswana, Lesotho and Swaziland, because (I suspect) they spoke the same languages as us (Sesotho, Setswana and SiSwati are all official languages in South Africa and spoken by many including myself). We also had relatives there and even visited over the December holidays. At a sub-conscious level, this created familiarity of culture and language which resulted in a perceived safety and a comfort zone, while on the other hand it was almost unheard of for someone from

Soweto to say, "I am going to Zimbabwe for a holiday". In addition, the framing of language used to describe countries north of the Limpopo carried connotations of sheer ignorance. It was common (to an extent even now) to hear people in South Africa say, "Those people from Africa", as if South Africa was outside the continent. It almost felt like those of us who had not travelled outside of South Africa into other parts of the continent had this imaginary ocean that divided us from the rest of the continent and its people. This type of ignorance can partly explain the xenophobia, or in particular, Afrophobia, that we have experienced in recent years. The fact that this negative attitude was directed at our African brothers and sisters as opposed to foreigners from countries in Europe or America points to a deeper problem of negative connotations attached to what it means to be African. The question may arise: 'What is African identity?'

In his key note address at the 30th commemoration of Steve Biko's death, former President Thabo Mbeki cited a passage from a book *Decolonising the Mind* by Kenyan novelist and author Ngugi wa Thiong'o, describing a stormy debate that once took place in the University of Nairobi. Ngungi says: "Three African lecturers and researchers at the university questioned the underlying assumption that English tradition and the emergence of modern West were the central root of Kenya's and Africa's consciousness and cultural heritage. They rejected the underlying notion that Africa was an extension of the modern West. Then followed the crucial rejoinder: If there is a need for a study of the historic continuity of a single culture, why can't this be African? Why can't African literature be at the centre so that we can view other cultures in relationship to it?" Mbeki concluded by saying, "This raises the question - what is African culture? What constitutes African identity, the opposite of the negative stereotype of ourselves which colonialism and racism presented to the African child so that he or she tended to find solace only in close identification with the white society?"

The above phenomenon played itself over and over again in my childhood years in Soweto. A higher status was clearly attached to arbitrary things; like geographical location, accent, the shade of one's skin - where lighter was always better. Such sentiment emerged all the time in subtle ways. I remember a particular set of twins in my neighbourhood. One was light in complexion and the other darker. Everyone picked up and doted on the lighter one, saying: "Oh how cute! She is so beautiful!", while totally ignoring the other. Such painful and **damaging bias was normalised literally from birth**.

While we held biases and stereotypes towards people from the neighbouring African countries, we also found other ways to stereotype one another. Of South Africa's nine main African linguistic groups, those who spoke Tshivenda and Xitsonga (then referred to as 'Shangaan') were considered inferior: supposedly darker, they were deemed less sophisticated, less everything. I have no idea where that stereotype came from – I just got onto that train without even checking its station of origin. I recall an incident when I was about 15 years old. Headed for an outing, I had dressed in a colourful outfit. A friend took one look and said, "Don't wear that, you look like a Shangaan". The Tsonga people were said to mix too many colours and lack fashion sense. I remember clearly how I deliberately stayed away from that outfit after that. I was proud to not be too dark. It is painful and embarrassing to think about that now, but this should be a reminder to all of us how these messages are passed on to children and can remain as their 'truth' unless there is a willingness to 'unlearn' the lies and confront these early messages.

While we maintained distinct pecking orders based on subtle differences in shades of black skin or inside knowledge concerning which part of Soweto a person came from, we meanwhile subscribed to a collective view of white people – whom most of us knew not at all. We competed in telling each other stories of how clever white people were, why they were 'bosses', how they always found solutions to complex problems. In our stories, all white people were clever. They were all smart. They were all rich. And they would rather allow a dog to sleep inside the house in bad weather than to shelter a black person for even a single night, because they were *all* racist.

So those are some of the narratives I picked up in my early years. And those early narratives – even when later proven ridiculous – tend to retain a powerful hold on our minds until we decide to do something and rewrite them. Yes, it can be done; we cannot hide behind "you can't teach an old dog new tricks" anymore. If one is willing to do the work, much can be achieved. Neuro-imaging research tells us that by age six, children's implicit attitudes and impressions are already formed. All experiences thereafter are filtered through the paradigms we learn as children. Absorbing the multi-layered subliminal messages surrounding us – from our communities, from our families, from the media – the neuro-pathways of our brains build stories. Like tracks laid for a train, it becomes not just normal that these narratives are 'the way', but unfathomable that any other route was ever possible. This is why the role of parents, teachers and others in positions of authority is critical in modelling positive behaviour, by challenging statements that denigrate those who are different or seen to have a lower status than us.

Transformation is the process of consciously rerouting one's pathways in order to find new truths. The process is both internal and external. At an internal level we must first recognise that our brains have learned a lot of nonsense that we must unlearn. At the same time, however, that nonsense continues to manifest externally in our interactions with others. Wherever we are on our transformation journey, we interact with others from the starting point of the baggage that we all carry. Packed by our parents, schools, media and communities before we had any say or even knew where we were going, that baggage is filled with narratives and ideas of what is 'normal'. Understand that every one of us carries this baggage (I call it a suitcase) and it continues to be repacked, even in our adulthood.

I got my first wake-up call about the contents of my own 'suitcase' the year I received my Matric results. Of my school's approximately 120 Matric students, I can recall only four of us receiving Matric exemptions, meaning we passed with the requirements necessary to apply to a university. It was my good friend Khanya, two Tsonga-speaking classmates and myself. In an instant, that narrative about Shangaans, so firmly cemented in my mind, was proven a ridiculous fabrication. I also recall that those Tsonga-speaking students scored particularly high in maths, which was my worst subject. For the first time I began to see my own ignorance. The whole episode sounds so obvious and perhaps patronising now, but it was such a wake-up call for me at the time.

Looking back on those dynamics – pockets of which sadly continue today – it is important to understand them in the context of the damage the apartheid system has done. As a young black person in that system you got so locked into your own nothingness that you just wanted to be better than someone else. So even if you were all regarded as lowly, within the lowliness, you said, "I'm a better low person than you". It was that kind of a thing. So that is what we did: try and instil a sense of better-than in ourselves. In fact, **human beings are forever striving to be better**. Overall this impulse creates a lot of good, but unfortunately it can and often does come at someone else's expense. As long as you can feel you have something that elevates you – gives you a higher rank than somebody else – that desire to be better is somewhat satisfied. Yet Noble Prize winner Ernest Hemingway showed his wisdom when he said, "There is nothing noble about being superior to your fellow man. True nobility is being superior to your former self". Growing up, I had the fortune of being in a 'better than' position. I do not say this in arrogance – in fact you could say it was God's unmerited favour in the form of the mother I was born to.

My mother, my trailblazer

MASEBEDI MOLEFI was born in 1935 in Mafikeng in the North West Province. She was a tall and confident woman. Strict but with an open and generous heart, she always gathered family around her. She loved her children fiercely and kept us close. She was also a real trendsetter. I'm not sure if she intended it or it just happened that way, but she was always three steps ahead of her peers. In 1975 she bought her own car. At the time it was difficult for a woman to even get a driver's license, yet here was my mother driving a bright red Ford Capri, a car whose sleek lines made it a popular ride. Everyone knew my mother's car. People would see her and say: "Who is this woman who can drive?" Her response? "What stops black women from owning cars?" My mother always communicated to me that nothing is impossible.

Although she only had a Matric, my mother expected me to get a degree. Instilling the value of books and education in me from a young age, she encouraged me to visit the Dube Library[1]. In the days before it was burnt out, I was constantly borrowing books, Dr Seuss being among my favourites. I remember being attracted by the cover, with many red hats stacked on top of another – *The Cat in the Hat* – I thought it was so funny. Every evening I knew I had to read a chapter of a book, and by the time I was eight I had fully adopted a culture of reading. Meanwhile, family discussions focused

---

[1] Although many Soweto townships did not have libraries, Dube, which was established in 1954 to accommodate a more exclusive 'middle-class', had such facilities. It was also home to wealthy and well-known people like Richard Maponya, Dr Nthato Motlana and Felicia Mabuza-Suttle.

on getting a degree and owning a car. My mother wanted me to be a social worker because that was one of the few jobs for women where you got a car from the government. A woman having her own car was a constant narrative at home. I cannot understate the role that conversations in a house have in shaping a child. The conversations in our house told me I would have a degree and a car. And so what might have seemed unattainable to neighbours or friends seemed not only achievable, but a natural progression that I did not question.

Of course it helped that success was modelled around me. Compared to the average white person at the time, my family had little, but within our community we were regarded as better off. My mother was an entrepreneur, selling clothes that she bought wholesale from connections she had made working as a factory seamstress years before. In those days, my father Albert worked as a messenger at De Beers in the Industrial Diamond Division. As my mother's business selling clothes became more successful, our house was renovated with 'big windows'. It sounds strange now, but during those years in the township, having big glass windows meant you were well off. We also had a full bathtub in a bathroom with beautiful tiles. And our house always had electricity, while most others did not. My mother loved beautiful things, and in the house she endeavoured to create a different environment. "Find a way" was her slogan.

In 1977, ours was one of the first houses in the neighbourhood to acquire a television set. In those days, boxing and soccer were most popular among township folks. Whenever sporting events were on, my house would fill to capacity – neighbours, cousins, anyone could come. The **spirit of abundance** was very evident in my mother. When space would run out inside, she would push the curtains back and all the kids would sit in the yard, watching whatever was showing on TV. The two events where the house was overflowing with people was the boxing match between Big John Tate and Kalie Knoetze, and later with Gerrie Coetzee. This was right in the middle of the apartheid years and almost everyone in Soweto was rooting for Big John Tate, who was a tall African American boxer from Tennessee in the USA. When he won both matches, the noise from my house and the hooting cars and the jubilation of children and adults in the streets of Soweto were something to marvel at; it was as if John Tate did something to bring justice and to defeat apartheid.

Over the years I observed that after leaving employment in the factories, my mother did much better financially. The house was always full of nice food – even cheese. It was just normal yellow cheese, but in the township it was a real luxury and my mother always welcomed the other kids to share – yes, cheese was a big deal. Kids would say, "Ah, you are rich, you have a TV, your mom has a car. Your fridge is always full of nice food". But it came with excitement, not jealousy. My mother filled our house with a sense of communal sharing, of connection to others. I liked that she had a big heart. I never used to believe it but there is a belief in my Setswana culture that if you name your child after someone, they tend to emulate or portray the same traits as that person. I named my daughter Masebedi after my mother and I can see almost exactly the same qualities of abundance and giving in her. Sometimes we do not take to heart the teachings of our grandparents; I am grateful that in this case, that belief turned to be true.

For all of her generosity and trailblazing, my mother was not a pioneer when it came to the messages she conveyed about race. I remember how she used to scold my brothers and me when we were being loud, telling us we sounded "like coloureds". This despite the fact that her closest friend Babsie – whose house in Eldorado Park we visited, whose children we played with, and whose extended family we interacted with a lot – was coloured. She was adamant that this assertion did not by any means include her friend Babsie. This is no different from someone saying to me "black people are lazy, but not you Nene, you are a better black". These stories demonstrate that bias has no logic and it can even be delusional to all of us who exhibit this behaviour. While this was said about coloured people, there were many subtle utterances that pointed to us aspiring to be coloured. For example, there was a popular song we sang at township weddings saying "tswang tswang le mmoneng, ngwana o tshwana le le Coloured"- loosely translated, it means come out and see her. The bride is so beautiful, she looks like a coloured person. So on the one hand you chastise your children to not behave like coloured people, but on the other hand you aspire to be like them.   My father's messages about race were different but equally unhealthy, expressing a blanket reverence for whites. You could hear it in the way he spoke, using phrases like, "A white man is clever... this is what they do..." Years later – long after my dad had retired from De Beers – we were chatting and I told him that his former employer was my client. "Are you saying *you* stand in front of senior leadership? Right there on 45 Main

Street?" he said, astounded by this unthinkable scenario. His inability to fathom how I might not only be upstairs in the top boardroom, but actually standing at the front presenting, brought tears to my eyes.

I would love to say that my parents opened my eyes to the discrimination and injustice around us, but the truth is they were just busy trying to survive – taking what the system dished out and all the while unthinkingly packing our bags with the stereotypes they had inherited from their parents and environments.

My mother's daughter: the importance of finishing

MOST OF WHAT I INHERITED from my mother I cherish to this day. She may not have been an activist, but when it came to our education, my mother's determination and focus were radical. From 1974-77, I attended Standards 1-5 (the equivalent of Grades 3-7) at St John's Berchmans Catholic School in Orlando East, Soweto. It was a chaotic era, which came to a head during the Soweto Uprisings of 1976. A series of protests organised by school children against the use of Afrikaans as the medium of instruction in government schools, the Soweto Uprising was a massive turning point in the struggle to take down apartheid.

I still recall the first day of the uprising on 16 June 1976. I was in Standard 3. Schools had closed early because of the danger in the townships, and my younger brother and I were making our way to the bus that would take us home. It was winter and we were both wearing red leather coats. On that day, bullets were literally flying around us. People were running, kids throwing bricks, police chasing them. Helicopters filled the sky. I remember a stone hitting my brother in the back of his red leather coat. I thought it was a bullet. We ran, just making it to the bus, which got us home safely.

For months following the uprising, many schools remained closed. At the time I remember a lot of my friends stopped going to school. It got comfortable to stay at home. Meanwhile, I continually heard the words 'education', 'don't drop it', and 'finish'. The seemingly simple practice of going to school and writing exams had become risky and dangerous in those days, but my mother was determined to prevent external circumstances from stealing my future. I learned then that there are always a million things urging you to throw in the towel, but having just one person to remind you of your sense of purpose can make all the difference.

But then one day that person was gone. I was 16 years old when my mother died from a blood clot. It was very fast and sudden. I was in Standard 9 (Grade 11) and in the middle of writing exams when it happened – I had written my other subjects and had only math and geography remaining. I could not imagine how I would get through. But then I heard her voice saying, "Education, just aim for it". So I wrote my last two exams between the time she died and was buried. Something in me had to do it. Looking back I see that was God's grace in my life.

After my mother's funeral, I recalled an incident that took place almost exactly a year before. I had visited a classmate's house in Meadowlands zone 2 where my school was situated. It had come up in our conversation that both her parents had died and she lived with her grandmother. "How do you survive without a mother? Who buys your clothes?" I honestly could not imagine how she survived without parents. Her situation was so removed from me and I had felt so sorry for her. And now here I was, one year later, also without parents. After my mother died, my father left my brothers and me to live full-time with his other family. We had always known about my father's other family, and until my mother's death, he had split his time between our households. But his sudden departure after her death forced me to learn overnight how you live without parents. Just like that, my life changed drastically. But as it has always been in my life, God's grace abounds. Without even thinking about it, I continued on my mother's path. One of the most important lessons I had learned from her is that **whatever the circumstances, you can make it**. Not only can you make it, you also can succeed without even making too much noise about it.

A BIG PART OF MAKING IT, despite the circumstances, is prayer and hard work. But another big part is learning how to ask for and accept help. It was a difficult time for learners at that time and my mother was constantly looking for better schools to enable me to finish my matric. I changed schools three times after completing my primary school. I attended Setilo Secondary School in Mareetsane, a small village in the North West Province, then went to Orlando West High School (popularly known as Matseke) in Soweto, and finally settled at Meadowlands High School where I completed Grades

10-12[2]. We didn't have a maths or science teacher in our final and most critical Grade 12 year. In the days when he was still around, my dad sometimes brought me old Matric papers or exams from 'white schools'. Especially when looking at the maths and science questionnaires, this combination of envy and astonishment would wash over me – there were people my age that actually understood these things? It seemed so unfair.

Despite having no maths and science teachers in our final year, we were expected to write these subjects just like everyone else in the country, so I spent most weekends of my Matric year at the Wits (University of Witwatersrand) campus in Braamfontein, where white students taught us a condensed version of the maths and science curriculum. If you missed one weekend you missed a lot. Between school from Monday to Friday, and these extra lessons on the weekends, I never had a rest that year. It was incredibly demanding, and I had to have the presence of mind to really want it, as no one at home was pressing for it. My dad had left by then, and my mother was gone.

Those weekend lessons were so defining for me. I started becoming friends with people who were serious about school. There were about seven of us who went religiously to Wits. A lot of others gave up. I still remember that one of the most passionate Wits tutors was always telling us, "You can make it in life!" I am so grateful thinking back to those dedicated students who gave up their weekends to teach us. They thought we were just coming for extra lessons – that we were joking or exaggerating when we said we had no maths and science teachers. A lack of teachers in township schools didn't make headlines back then.

IT WAS A SUNNY DAY in December 1982, a year after my mom had passed away. I still remember waking up that morning and going to check *The World* newspaper (now *Sowetan*) to see if my name was among those listed in the Matric results[3]. It is hard to explain my excitement when I saw my name with an asterisk next to it. Not only had I passed, but I had also received an exemption, which meant I had qualified for University entrance. Although

---

[2] Known then as Forms 3-5

[3] In South Africa the results of the Matric exam, or high school diploma qualification, are printed in the local newspapers, which is how students first discover if they have passed or failed. An "exemption" means a student's score qualifies for university admission.

the Matric results were published in the paper, you still had to fetch the actual report from school. Walking to the taxis that morning I had visions of my mother. I've never walked so confidently in my life. I remember crossing paths with an elderly woman, who stopped me and said, ""My child, I love the way you walk. Where are you going?" It was the shortest walk to the taxis ever. I so wished my mother could have been there.

By then I was living with my aunt Ous Sasa and my uncle Victor. In fact, Ous Sasa is my mother's cousin. In African culture, one hardly uses the word cousin, so we just called them sisters. They had had a lot in common – Ous Sasa was also an entrepreneur who sold clothes – and we had always been very close. Ous Sasa was and is a beautiful soul. To this day if I say I'm going home, I mean her house. Thanks to this generous woman and her husband, my Matric exemption meant something. Just six months after my mother had passed, Ous Sasa told me it was time to apply to universities, assuring me that she would pay my fees. She did not need to tell me twice. I applied to the traditionally black universities of Fort Hare and the University of the North, and was accepted at Fort Hare. I didn't even consider applying anywhere else. As far as I was concerned, university meant the black universities. That was where we belonged, or at least that was the thinking at the time. And now, university acceptance and Matric exemption in hand, it was time to go realise my mother's dreams for me.

INSIGHTS & TIPS

From this early period, one of the biggest lessons to emerge is the importance of childhood narratives and how they shape your biases and views of people who are different from you. This points to our role as adults, and how the work of diversity and inclusion is not only for the workplace, but starts at home.

Unzip your 'suitcase' and rewrite negative childhood narratives

1. **Start with yourself**

Practical Tips

- Like so many journeys, the most difficult part of the transformation journey is choosing to take the first step. That means having the readiness and willingness to unlearn the things we were taught by those we love and respect.

- Begin the process of opening your baggage, sifting through it, and removing what does not serve you, is hurtful to others, and was packed without your permission. This job is yours and yours alone.

- Think about the first time you encountered or had experiences of anyone different to you, e.g. race, gender, language, religion? What impact if any did that interaction have on your awareness of yourself and of the other?

- Ask yourself: what was I taught or what did I pick up about those who are 'different' from me? For example, what was I taught about people of _____ race group? What was I taught about men/women? What did I come to believe about people of a different sexual orientation or different religion than my own?

- Think about how these hidden beliefs have affected how you relate to people who are different from you. Have they come out in things you have said or done?

2. **Question the messages you transmit at home**

Practical Tips

- Continue to ask yourself what messages you were fed, and what messages you feed your own children. These can be both verbal and non-verbal.

- How do you speak to the people who work in your house (e.g. cleaner, gardener, repairmen, etc.)? What tone do you use?

- Do your tone and/or actions contradict the words you say, i.e. you can tell your child "respect is important, you must respect the helper because she is older than you", but if you use a demeaning tone when speaking to her (or about her to your partner), or if your child sees you doing things like giving her different utensils to use, then your body language and behaviour will override your words. *What you say is theory; what you do is real.*

3. **Beware the power of subliminal messages**

Practical Tips

- Many of our early messages are picked up from our environment or from the media, not just from direct messages spoken to us by our parents.

- Pay attention to the types of media you allow your children to watch or consume. The media (including seemingly "harmless" cartoons and video games) can be extremely violent and full of prejudice, even if within age restrictions. For example, if video games demonstrate that men always get their way by being violent, that becomes a story that is formed in a child's mind. These types of subliminal messages are powerful and reinforced all the time.

- In the workplace, observe what news station or channel is always on the office televisions. What pictures are on the walls? Do they portray diversity or only one particular race group or gender?

4. Challenge second-hand stories

Practical Tips

- Intentionally look for disconfirming data to counteract early messages and stereotypes (e.g. about white people, Africans, males, gay people, foreign nationals, etc.). Disconfirming data are the examples and experiences that contradict the dominant stereotypes.

- Once you find disconfirming data, raise awareness about it and challenge the common narrative.

- Take deliberate steps to educate yourself about cultures and stories that are not readily accessible to you, e.g. read African literature, or reference and profile African authors, stories and inventions that demonstrate that thought leadership does not only reside in Western countries.

- Help your children or peers to also see that the early messages they were fed are not all true. People might resist this kind of conversation to begin with, but that is usually a sign that it is exactly the kind of thing they need to hear.

5. Take our role as adults seriously

Practical Tips

- Unzip your suitcase: keep what is useful and take out (unlearn) what does not serve you and replace it with new truths.

- Be conscious and careful not to perpetuate the same negative messages with children who look up to you.

- Actively point out disconfirming data to young ones; when there is a stereotype about a group of people, look for as many instances where that same person/group does the opposite, and point it out to children so they can form a new reality.

Applying the lesson of transmitting messages at work

Transformation can be a very difficult process. Like any challenging goal, one must first confront one's internal barriers and be determined, focused, and willing to work and sacrifice for it.

6. Question the messages you transmit at work

 Practical Tips

- What messages are you feeding your employees/co-workers? Again, these can be both verbal and non-verbal.

- Look at how your messages and actions line up. Do they? For example, at work, if every time a black or female candidate is presented for appointment and the first statement you utter is: "But this should be on merit", you need to ask yourself if you say the same thing when a white or male candidate is proposed. If not, it is time to hold up the mirror and question your assumptions and the messages you continue to transmit.

7. Stand up, show resilience and be ready for discomfort

Practical Tips

- Accept the reality that no one else can do this for you.

- Discomfort is part of growth; see it as an opportunity to learn valuable lessons.

- When your situation is difficult or uncomfortable, remember you can ask for and accept help from others.

8. Don't lump people together

Practical Tips

- It can be frustrating to see people who seem not to care about what you care about. I felt this way in school about the kids who seemed not to care about continuing to study. But do not allow yourself to generalise as a result – for example, thinking that all township children are lazy, ungrateful, and not serious about their studies. Such a generalisation is just a show of total ignorance of the complexity of township life. In the same vein, believing that all white people are selfish, uncaring, and racist is incredibly limited and simply untrue.

- In every group of people that you think you know something about, there is so much hunger for change and growth. Just because you do not see or understand it, does not mean it is not there.

Chapter 2

LEARNING CURVES

Social differentials and micro-inequities (1983-1985)

We now accept that learning is a life-long process of keeping abreast with change. The most pressing task is to teach people how to learn.

Nelson Mandela

ARRIVING AT FORT HARE'S beautiful campus in 1983, I was astonished by the sudden freedom and independence that came with having no adults around. At the same time, there were a lot of us from Soweto. With 99% of us in 'res', or student housing, Fort Hare quickly felt like a familiar second home. We did what all first-year university students do: party, socialise, and test our boundaries. Without teachers and parents breathing down our necks anymore, it was now up to us to succeed or derail. It was quite a learning curve, but for me passing was never negotiable. It was paramount that I not disappoint my aunt.

Meanwhile, I was easing into the atmosphere of the Eastern Cape. The province of activists, despite or maybe because of still being the Ciskei homeland[4], my new environment was opening my eyes politically. Although the 1976 uprisings had woken me up to the way things were changing, I was still so young at that time – only 12 years old – and had not really understood the stakes in fighting the system.

It was at Fort Hare that my political consciousness was born. I was 18 and finally grasping the depth of what the government had done to our parents and black people in general. Realising how many people had died, and what really happened in the aftermath of 1976, I suddenly saw why we had to stand up and fight. It was at that time that I felt a sense of loss for my parents. By virtue of not being activists, they had been in a way a part of the system, albeit as unwilling participants. For my part, I could no longer afford to be ignorant, nor did I want to be.

---

[4] An apartheid government policy, the homeland system set aside "territories" (or homelands, also known as Bantustans or black states) for black people in South Africa and Namibia (then South West Africa), with the goal of creating ethnically homogenous "nation states" that could have varying degrees of autonomy from South Africa. They were abolished and reabsorbed into South Africa after the fall of apartheid in 1994.

The older and more politically active students at Fort Hare were constantly speaking out against the homeland system. The rest of us were a captive audience, easy to conscientise and always ready to sing those exciting songs about OR Tambo coming to liberate us. Meanwhile, Lennox Sebe, the Ciskei homeland leader, treated our university as one of his pet projects. He would come to campus with the Ciskei police, chasing and beating us, targeting activist leaders. I was beaten once, but I kept returning, loving being part of something so vital, something so much bigger than me.

In the end, though, I knew why I was at Fort Hare. The focus I had learned from my mother stayed with me despite the strength of activism's pull. That period in Fort Hare forced me to find a balance between freedom and responsibility. I wanted to be part of fighting the system, but I also had to ensure that I finish my studies and fulfil my responsibilities to myself and to my aunt who was paying my university fees. It was not always easy, as there were so many voices and ideas about what it meant to be part of the struggle. People had strong opinions about how change needed to come about. For me, completing my education also felt like a political choice. But **finding the balance between ideals and ambition** is a question never perfectly answered, and is something that must constantly be renegotiated along one's journey.

As I neared completion of my degree in Social Work, I knew I wanted to carry on to do an Honours degree[5]. Many of my friends were staying at Fort Hare to do theirs. Having enjoyed the growth of being far from home, I had studied and read about other universities and thought: why not try something else? So I applied to do an Honours degree in Social Work at the University of Cape Town (UCT). Some people thought I was crazy. We called UCT the 'white liberal university'. It seemed unattainable for people like us. Looking back I see so clearly how even as we were in the midst of fighting for freedom, our own minds could hold us back. I had never been to Cape Town, but I fantasised about UCT because it was in Cape Town, a faraway place with a reputation for being very beautiful, but also very white and elitist. I think I had my mother's 'why not?' attitude about that latter detail.

---

[5] In South Africa, an Honours degree is a one-year post-graduate degree, done after receiving one's Bachelors, which is normally completed in three years.

I was elated when I received the news that I had been accepted for my Honours at UCT. I was going to Cape Town! I had no idea what to expect, and I was also not sure how I would pay for it. My aunt had agreed to pay for my transport to Cape Town and to help me with res, but I did not have a cent to pay the significantly higher tuition. I wrote to the university administration asking about bursaries, and applied for everything I could. As has happened so many times in my life, God's favour arrived just at the right moment. During the second month after school started I received a bursary from the New England Board of Higher Education in the USA, covering my tuition.

Stranger in a strange land

ARRIVING IN CAPE TOWN in 1986 was like stepping into a new country. The newness came at me in multiple layers. I was 21 years old, and until then had never interacted with white people on any personal or meaningful basis, with the exception of the tutors at Wits. Now the majority of my peers were white. Even Cape Town's black townships felt incredibly different. The predominant language was isiXhosa, which, having just come from the Eastern Cape, I understood, but the language diversity I was accustomed to in Soweto was absent. In its place were English or Afrikaans.

Most of the people who became my friends mainly came from outside of Cape Town: Rustenburg, Mafikeng, Pretoria, Soweto and other parts of Johannesburg. We were all curious to explore our new surroundings. Cape Town's beaches were a major attraction, but not being from a coastal area, I always had the impression that everyone in this place was constantly on holiday. 'When do these people work?' I wondered. When we did go to the beach we were rowdy. We would hang around the open boot of a car and have a party. White people would look at us like we were taking their peace. That was not done. In Cape Town you could feel how you were supposed to honour some set of unwritten rules concerning where white people didn't want black people to go. But we were emboldened by our student mentality that challenged everything. Bold poses notwithstanding, I could see that it wasn't easy for black people to fit into things in this city, and in fact rebellion was a form of survival.

I also remember having the distinct impression that black people in Cape Town had bought into the story that they didn't belong there. Both white and black people seemed so defined by where they lived in Cape Town. I suppose that kind of thing can become a self-fulfilling prophecy. A lot of what I observed while living in Cape Town fell under that category – my own behaviour being no exception. And so although I was aware of Cape Town's famous beauty, I saw it as unattainable or not meant for people like me. Being in Cape Town was like looking through a magazine whose pages I would never be in. Thinking back, it is a shock to realise how casually my younger self accepted these things. I was a student wearing my rebel hat, but I had my friends and we didn't dwell on the negatives, and I knew I would leave soon enough.

Social differentials and micro-inequities

IN THE MEANTIME, however, the inequalities in my new environment were affecting my outcomes as a student, and that hurt. Unlike Fort Hare, where many of us came from a similar background, the **social differentials** at UCT were very pronounced. By social differentials I mean the gap that exists between different race or gender groups, based on the disadvantages attached to different backgrounds. These gaps are often linked to social roles and whether one is seen as an insider or outsider, which in turn often corresponds to opportunities and outcomes.

For example, you can have two students in the same class with the same lecturers; one, the outsider, is from Mafikeng, and the other one, the insider, is from Bantry Bay[6]. The one from Mafikeng is the first person in his family to go to university. He is struggling with a place to stay and does not have enough money for food. He comes to lectures often having travelled far, having had little sleep and not enough food. The student from Bantry Bay has a car, a personal computer, a living allowance from parents who are both professionals with degrees, and he never worries about where his fees will come from. Both students show up to lectures to receive what is called 'equal' access to education, but these social differentials show just how unequal a notion this is. Later, social roles – such as who will be chosen

---

[6] Bantry Bay is one of Cape Town's most affluent suburbs, located along the section of Atlantic coast dubbed "millionaire's mile" by real estate agents. Mafikeng is the capital of the North West Province, a provincial town that is a mix of the rural and semi-rural, with areas of extreme poverty and high levels of unemployment. It was in the surrounding area of Verdwaal where four children aged 2 to 9 died of starvation in late 2011, their bodies found on the road where they had collapsed in search of food.

to intern at a prestigious firm – will be assigned. And after that, first job opportunities will come along. More often than not we see how these social differentials continue to influence who will be selected for which roles and jobs, even if both students had access to what was supposed to be an equal education.

While sleeping without a plate of food was not one of my personal experiences, I had my share of experiences with social differentials. In my honours class at UCT, our major assignment was a community profile in which we researched and analysed institutions and notable residents in order to write a complete history of that community. I chose Woodstock, a historically working class and mixed-race neighbourhood just a few kilometres from Cape Town's city centre. Woodstock appealed to me because it was not your traditional black township, but neither was it a typical rich white area. Interviews were a key component of the assignment – speaking with the librarian, the oldest person in the community, the police station commander, hospital superintendent, and so on. We had three months to complete the whole assignment, a timeframe I originally thought generous, but two weeks in I still hadn't managed to set up a single appointment. I was really struggling.

Meanwhile, for the very first time I had become friendly with a white person. Kathy[7] was also in my honours class. We often sat next to one another in class and would chat. We weren't close friends, but we were friendly. At some point it came up that I had never been to a white person's house, and she invited me over. I was intrigued: visiting with her family in Bishops Court, I still remember my surprise at how casually she related to her mother, who was very welcoming and easy going. Unexpectedly, I found their home not so different from either the home I had grown up in or my aunt's house. We also had big TVs, nice kitchen appliances, and so on. The one shocking thing to me was the garden – you could have put five houses there. I remember thinking it was such a waste, wondering if they actually sat in that huge garden every day. It's funny looking back on it now, as I also have a big garden that I only occasionally use. It's nice to have, but I would struggle to explain exactly why if someone asked. Anyway, when it was time to sit down to dinner I remember this formal situation with everyone around the table

---

[7] Name changed

asking me questions. The questions themselves were not intimidating – just polite 'getting to know you' conversation – but at the time it felt like an interview session. I was relieved when it was over.

Not long after that dinner I confided in Kathy about how I was struggling with our assignment, only to discover that she had already seen about 11 people and was almost done. When I asked how she had managed to work so quickly, she told me that her dad's PA helped set up her appointments. She was in no way boasting, just honestly answering my question with no awareness of the impact her answer had on me. I went to my room and cried. I had been calling people to make appointments, but had so far only succeeded with one. An unbelievable feeling of hopelessness consumed me. I felt like I didn't even know who to approach to ask for help.

You see, all the people I was trying to meet were white. Picture trying to get an appointment with the police station commissioner, who is white, the librarian, the longest serving shop owner, the oldest resident etc., all of whom, in Cape Town in those days – even in racially mixed Woodstock – were mainly white. Just picking up a phone and explaining myself already spelled defeat. Some heard my accent and would put the phone down before I could finish. Others kept saying, "What are you saying? Who are you?" I would say that I was a UCT student, but I could already hear they were not interested. Others would say yes, they would come back to me, but they never came back. So that was what I was dealing with.

At the time I was interning at the Woodstock Hospital, also as part of my degree. I reported to an Afrikaans-speaking woman who was the head of social work. When I told her what was happening she said, "You should have told me!" Just like that, she picked up the phone and called the commissioner of the police station, saying, "Do me a favour...", and things started moving. I can say she used her power, her whiteness, to set up those appointments for me.

The ease with which she helped me also turned the mirror back to me. I had to ask what was happening in my head that had prevented me from asking her for help sooner. Did I actually think she would say no? I chastised myself for not speaking up earlier. Even after the appointments were made, I feared what I would say in the interviews, how I would come across, or that they would cancel on me. Remember some of those interviewees were the same people I had called who had turned me down or even hung up the phone. Although I now came with the 'backing' of the hospital social worker, I had been given a subtle but clear message: **'You are not worthy as you are'**. That message affected me a great deal.

In the end I finished the assignment just in time. All that remained was binding it. I recall how Kathy's assignment had graphs and colours. "My dad is doing it for me," she had said again, not realising how that sounded to me. The day we received our marks was when I really felt the gap – the social differentials between the two of us. I looked at the mark that she got (89%) and the one that I got (58%), and I can say without a string of a doubt that the difference was not because of more effort or intelligence from her side, or laziness or lack of passion from me. But the difficulty I had making those appointments — how it first slowed me down, and then affected my confidence when it came to the actual interviews — well, I have to admit there was a bit of bitterness inside of me. Kathy's assignment was beautiful, no doubt. I would also have given her that mark had I been the lecturer. But when I look at what she had at her disposal versus what I had, it felt unfair somehow. At the time I did not have a name for what happened, I just knew I was struggling and it hurt.

When people say things like, "But you were all at UCT in the same class with the same lecturers being taught the same thing", I want them to see how they are missing all the things that were not the same. On an obvious level there were the **micro-inequities**[8] that caused white authorities to immediately dismiss a black voice on the other end of the phone, and then there were actual material differences like a car to drive to interviews, or having a dad with the know-how and equipment to help produce a nice-looking final assignment.

But underneath all of that was yet another even more fundamental layer related to differences in one's general education preceding university. That is, the gap that results from the way a township child and a child from a 'rich suburb' are raised and educated. Being at UCT I was constantly made aware of how unprepared I was; how much my fellow students knew that I did not.

---

[8] Micro-inequities are subtle and devaluing messages of prejudice that are often unconscious on the part of the person transmitting them, but often impair or discourage performance for the person on the receiving end.

BEYOND THE DIFFERENCE IN MOTHER TONGUES, I could hear how other students used concepts that I was not familiar with. The richness of their English vocabulary also seemed to match what we were studying in our textbooks. For example, I remember hearing people talking about 'month-end budgets', 'strategy' or 'investments', and having no idea what they meant. I sometimes responded to my ignorance by making jokes: "Those ones are stingy, making budgets." But of course this just showed my lack of understanding of economics and how the world works. A lot of this knowledge is simply about familiarity with terminology – what words mean and how concepts function. Often these are things that you learn, or do not, at home.

Of course I had had conversations with my parents about work, but it was chalk and cheese from what someone like Kathy would have heard in terms of both depth and perspective. Even in her apparent trendsetting ways, my mother never mentioned such concepts. I heard a lot about my father's workplace, but his angle was from the point of view of being a clerk and messenger, not the director presenting in the boardroom. In my father's narratives, the world of work was always about the superiority of a white manager or white colleague. That said, I was fortunate to have had even those conversations. To this day in Soweto and most township households, many parents have to leave the house as early as 4am to take multiple forms of transport to get to jobs they only return from by 8 or 9pm. Because of this, children can go a whole week without seeing their parents. I was fortunate to have parents who didn't depend on public transport; we had time to sit and talk. All those dreams my mother had for me – she had time to share them.

Even so, the way I grew up, my parents' involvement in school life was almost zero. There was just no time. For my father in his low level position to say I need to leave early today because I'm going to see my child play sport or even to meet with a teacher – it was unimaginable. The more educated you are, the more you understand the importance of being in your child's school life. Our parents missed how important that was because it was not done. And this is assuming you had parents.

When I look at the plight of child-headed families in our townships and rural areas, it is so clear how the **cumulative effect of the surrounding circumstances** contributes to people giving up. Even for those who have someone paying basic school fees, if you do not have money for transport, food, or just the essentials, it is so easy to give up, never mind having conversations in your home about how to succeed. These kinds of social differentials are not just a thing of the past or observations from my university days. A large majority of black South African children still go through and feel the impact of various social differentials – many of which remain unchanged from my time – affecting their performance at school and later in the workplace.

This is why it is so frustrating – even for students now – when people see you in the same class, with the same lecturers, being taught the same thing, and they expect that the output should be the same. You obviously can't expect a professor to mark you based on different standards, but what would make a difference is if there was a level of awareness concerning what students are going through.

We underestimate the power of acknowledging the truth. There is such value in first recognising that these inequalities exist, and second asking if you can help. That kind of acknowledgement can make a dramatic difference to a person going through such an experience. Using the example of my assignment – had anyone openly acknowledged that the way I picked up the phone and called the police commissioner compared to the way a white student did would lead to different results – it really would have helped.

The most painful thing is when people deny that these inequalities exist. If people won't admit to these differences, it makes you – the person who is disadvantaged – reluctant to raise them for fear of being seen as someone who does not want to work hard. Kids can die a silent death in these situations. You enter this spiral of self-doubt, and instead of asking for help you rather suffer alone for fear of confirming someone else's stereotype of you.

This is what is meant when we talk about giving way to **stereotype threat**, a term coined by Claude Steel in his book, *Whistling Vivaldi*. Steel defined stereotype threat as "being at risk of confirming as true the negative stereotype of your group"[9]. For fear of 'proving' stereotypes about black

---

[9] Steele, C. 2010. *Whistling Vivaldi: and other clues to how stereotypes affect us.* New York: W.W. Norton & Company.

people (e.g. that they are not capable), many black students end up perpetuating what is called the **cycle of prejudice**: they will not seek help, instead suffering in silence and eventually dropping out – a result which ironically confirms the very stereotype that they were trying to avoid.

There are people who are quick to respond to all of this by pointing to the few people who are able to ask for help or make it through. Though you will always find exceptions, the critical mass is going through an experience that is linked to the **cumulative effect of past exclusions**. This is not to say that people who have been disadvantaged need to have things given to them on a plate, but there needs to be a much greater level of awareness.

IN THE MIDST OF MY ACADEMIC CONCERNS was a very real practical one. When I first arrived at UCT, many black students, including myself, were not able to live in res, or the on-campus student housing. This was not a problem faced by white students. "How can you accept black students but then not include them in res?", we asked. Most of us ended up living between 15 to 25 kilometres away from UCT, travelling daily to campus from Malunga Park in the township of Gugulethu or Baker House in Athlone. Studying at night was always a frustration, because although the library was open until 10pm, the only transport back to Malunga Park left campus much earlier. This was yet another disparity that black students had to deal with. I did not personally live in Malunga Park but rather in Langa Township with my other aunt, Aus Rose, who welcomed me in her house and made me part of the family with her husband Poni and my three cousins. The challenge of accessing the library was exactly the same for me as experienced by those students in Guguletu or Athlone.

But then, with the help of the well-known cleric and activist, Allan Boesak, students fought back. We marched on the streets of Rondebosch, got the administration's attention, and eventually many undergraduate students did get places in res. Since I was a post-graduate student I got a place in Glendower, which had about 50% black students. Having sorted out my living situation, I felt much more at home in Cape Town and was able to focus on my education and obtain the post-graduate certificate that would serve as a stepping stone to so many other things.

INCREASINGLY I RECOGNISE THE IMPORTANCE of education and the influence of the people closest to you. It sounds obvious but has to be mentioned. I remember during our Matric year my friend Khanya and I used to dream about university. Even though we did not know where the money would come from, when talking about the next year of our lives we only talked about university, never about what we would do if we stayed home. She also got into Fort Hare, and from the moment we got there, our focus was on completing our degrees.

At the same time, whenever I went home for holidays, I saw the gap growing with other friends. When I look at the people I grew up with, around 60% never went beyond Matric. I see where they are in life today: many struggling with alcoholism and a sense of helplessness. For a lot of them it started back in that period in 1976 when they stopped going to school, didn't write exams, and the culture of staying home took over. Most did not have mentors to take them out of that.

When I talk about social differentials, I'm not just talking about money, but also the surrounding environment that consumes you; the conversations you have, what you get exposed to, someone to hold your hand when you are about to sink. Growing up there was no difference between those friends and me but for my mother's influence, which kept me in school in 1976, and thankfully kept me going after she died.

INSIGHTS & TIPS

My greatest insights from this period in my life come from the fact that despite being relatively privileged in the eyes of my friends in Soweto, I was still so disadvantaged in many ways, simply due to differences in my background: the school I went to and the type of education and socialisation I therefore received. I also gained insights about the power of mentors, hopeful conversations and allies throughout my learning journey.

How environments can disempower: social differentials and micro-inequities

Social differentials are the differences between people of different races, genders, or class groups, based on disadvantages attached to backgrounds. Micro-inequities are subtle, devaluing and recurring messages of prejudice that are often unconscious on the part of the person transmitting them, but often impair or discourage performance for the person on the receiving end. Anyone interested in true transformation must learn to recognise these things.

Pay attention to your own denial of, and/or behaviours around, micro-inequities

 Practical Tips

Ask yourself if you exhibit any of the following:

- Do you automatically doubt the work that is produced by someone because of his or her skin colour, gender or any other marker of diversity?

- Do you acknowledge an idea presented by different people in the same way?

- Do you ever:

  ◦ ignore an idea presented by one person, but praise the same idea when it comes from someone else?

  ◦ elevate the work or opinions of certain individuals over others who are working on the same project or in the same environment?

  ◦ dismiss some people's contributions and/or simply not listen to certain people?

- What is your body language saying when people speak to you? Do you:

  ◦ listen with arms closed, a frown on your face?

  ◦ sit in a way that excludes (with your back to someone, etc.)?

  ◦ look at your watch while someone is talking to you?

  ◦ type away at your keyboard while you are talking to someone?

  ◦ shake one person's hand and ignore another in the same team?

- Remember that micro-inequities are often hard to prove and easy to minimise.

The power of listening

Listening to people who have gone through difficult experiences or are experiencing exclusion or disadvantage is paramount.

Do not underestimate the power of the inner dialogue in someone's head

Practical Tips

- When people are excluded or struggling, they may want to ask for help but the messages in their heads tell them not to.

- Be aware that this person has to overcome the voice of an inner critic (self-doubt, etc.) to share his/her story, and may be worried that things could worsen after sharing.

- Recognise how much courage it can take for someone to speak up.

- Be honest and open: express your willingness to listen and learn from whatever a person might want to share with you.

- Recognise and tell the person sharing with you that you might 'say the wrong thing', and if so, to feel free to let you know.

Be aware of how you respond when someone raises an issue of micro-inequity or a social differential

Practical Tips

- Is your first instinct to say, "What's the big deal?" If so, check yourself and really reconsider what the person is saying.

- If you don't understand what the big deal is, ask questions with a desire to truly understand where this other person is coming from.

Walk a mile in someone else's shoes

Practical Tips

- We often hear stories of this in the workplace where managers are not aware of what their employees go through on a daily basis. For example, employees may have issues getting to work on time as they are relying on multiple taxis to get there. Management should not have different standards or condone issues like lateness, but encourage awareness and open communication about how to resolve or accommodate issues together.

Be aware of the influence of others

Practical Tips

- Remember that the people you surround yourself with have a major impact on your choices and views.

- Make an effort to be around people who challenge your unconscious biases and whose values you respect and admire. Inclusion and respect for diversity should ideally be one of those values.

- Talk about questions or matters of diversity and transformation with people from different backgrounds; it can be uncomfortable sometimes, but this is how we learn.

The quality of your listening determines the quality of the content a person can share

Practical Tips

Quality of listening means:

- **Don't interrupt.** If someone has had to gather courage to speak up, allow them to finish without interrupting. In contrast, if you've already asked me three questions before I finish one sentence, it changes my script and I am now responding to your questions instead of stating my case or telling my story.

- **Save your questions.** Questioning and probing can improve an outcome and show that you are listening, but save it until the person has been allowed to finish what they came to say.

- **Use your questions well.** In other words, use questions to ensure that you heard the other person correctly, not to show what you know.

- **It's not about you.** Don't be too quick to relate an experience that you think is similar to that of the person speaking; this can dilute the essence of the other person's story, putting the focus back on you.

- **Don't finish sentences.** Also avoid correcting the phrases or facts that the other person has included in his/her story.

Read a wider range of literature from different continents and cultures to counteract ignorance and limited perspectives

 ## Practical Tips

- Be intentional about searching for writers and research material from the broader African continent that will enable you to appreciate the knowledge and wisdom that sits there.

- Understand that some cultures place more emphasis on nuances beyond factual data. Be willing to be vulnerable and incorporate the mind, body and emotion as part of the learning journey. Ask questions to seek clarity and be willing to receive feedback that might not align with your world view.

Chapter 3

THE UNSUNG HERO BEHIND YOU

The power of unofficial mentors (1985-91)

Do a good deed and throw it into the sea.

Egyptian Proverb

Yvonne Herring (now Brewer), the head of social work at Cape Town's
Red Cross War Memorial Children's Hospital, asked if I would like to be
interviewed for a social work position. It was October and I hadn't even
written my final exams. I had heard of people calling a hundred places
looking for work, so you can imagine my excitement to interview for a job
I had not even applied for. Yvonne had done her homework, having gotten
my name from one of my lecturers at UCT. When we met she told me the
hospital didn't have a single black social worker. "You'll be the first one", she
said. I liked her transparency. "But I'll be here to support you", she added.
And just like that, I got my first job as the first black social worker at Red
Cross Children's Hospital.

I worked as a social worker in the Burns Unit from 1987-1988, which was
the hospital's busiest unit. With every Monday's intake of new patients, the
violence and abuse of small children that we saw was an eye opener for me.
If a doctor in casualty saw a child, a social worker had to be present, and
because a lot of abuse happens at night, I was regularly called in at all hours.
Everyone in that hospital was on call. We worked hard and I learned so much
– it was an excellent teaching hospital – but the trauma around our unit was
intense. In that madness, I was lucky to have a wonderful boss.

Yvonne[10] was a tall slender Afrikaans woman in her 30s. She had long
straight black hair and a thin face with a sharp nose. She always wore pants
and stylish flat shoes. In recruiting me, Yvonne very clearly recognised that
in addition to being the hospital's only black social worker, I was one of the
youngest on her team, and one of the few not from Cape Town. She saw
these things as requiring care, and often intervened on my behalf.

---

[10] In a funny coincidence, I was still going by the name Yvonne at school and work in those days.
Many black South Africans (then and now) have an English name that we use at school and at work,
and a real African name, which we use at home and with friends. Yvonne and I sharing the same
name initially caused a lot of confusion, and people took to saying, "The black Yvonne" or "The
white Yvonne". We then agreed that since all my friends and family called me Nene, I would use
Nene to minimise confusion. I have used my proper African name with everyone ever since.

Within the world of the hospital, I was learning about discrimination of a new type: that is, ranking by profession. Doctors were obviously the most important, followed by nurses, and then social workers, occupational therapists and physiotherapists were somewhere at the bottom. Right from the start, Yvonne took me by the hand to introduce me to all of the medical heads – in other words, the hospital's most highly ranked people. As she was introducing me, one doctor said in excitement, "At last we have someone who can speak an African language", to which Yvonne responded, "She is not an interpreter. She is a social worker, she is a professional". At the time I didn't understand the importance of that statement. You know, when you don't know what you don't know. That was me back then. In any case, after the introductions she told me to let her know if I had any trouble, but otherwise to "go for it".

Now it was up to me to establish my own relationships with the doctors and nurses. I remember going on ward rounds with the head of the Burns Unit, Professor Cecil Bloch, a very senior and respected doctor. Professor Bloch taught me how a ward round should run. He would not begin ward rounds unless everyone on his team was present, including a social worker. On a typical round he would stop and ask his whole team of doctors about a patient. Then he would look at me and say: "Okay Nene, do we discharge this patient? What is the home situation?" Here was Professor Bloch, asking my opinion, allowing everyone to listen to me. Because he was such a highly respected doctor, his attitude influenced how all the other doctors treated me.

This is a perfect example of a practice we encourage in diversity and inclusion work, that is, **using your rank, power, and position** to positively influence an environment and make another person's life easier. Professor Bloch's respect for my opinion also propelled me to always be prepared with the background of each and every patient. Although I don't think he necessarily intended it, Professor Bloch's confidence acted as a catalyst to start my own self-monitored **accelerated development** – or doing the catch-up work needed to operate at a higher level.

ALTHOUGH LACKING AFRICANS, the staff at Red Cross was relatively diverse – the nurses, other social workers, and occupational therapists were coloured, Indian and white. The cleaning staff were almost all coloured.

Looking back I can see that it was largely thanks to Yvonne's interventions and leadership that I felt a part of things without too much trouble.

One issue that came up repeatedly at the hospital was brought on by the lack of African-language ability among the medical staff. That meant that whenever we had an African patient whose family did not speak English or Afrikaans, I was the nearest professional who could communicate with them, and as a result, every floor sought my help in translating. In my naivety I didn't mind, thinking that I was just being helpful with a skill I had, and I felt for the families as well, but echoing her introductions to the medical heads when I first arrived, Yvonne insisted that I refrain from translating.

At first I didn't understand what the big deal was, but then she educated me, making me see how in the bigger picture my 'helpfulness' actually prevented me from doing my own work, which would feed or perpetuate perceptions people might have had about me as the only African social worker. She explained that even if people meant well, I had gone to university just like them, and I should **operate at the level of my qualification**. Looking back now it seems so foolish of me not to have seen that, but we all go through our 'teachable moments' in life.

By using me as a translator, she explained, the hospital could stall on what they should rather be doing, which was to employ African nurses and doctors who could treat patients and convey medical information to them and their families.

Yvonne taught me so many things, fighting battles for me that I didn't even see. At our team's monthly meetings someone always had to take minutes. The first time it was my turn, my colleagues patronised me, saying, "Don't worry, someone else can take minutes". But Yvonne made me part of the team, saying, "No, it's Nene's turn". Fresh from university, I wrote everything down verbatim. This one says this, that one says that. Afterwards, when everyone else was gone, Yvonne sat me down and gave me feedback. First she acknowledged me for writing so quickly, really giving me accolades and making me feel good. Only after that she said, "Next time, don't write everything everyone is saying, just the resolutions". In this way, she indirectly coached and mentored me.

This is **the difference between spoon feeding and mentoring**. Yvonne gave me feedback on my work (in this case, the minutes). She taught me the principles of what was needed, but I was always the one who had to do the work. She guided but never did my work for me. Sometimes you'll hear managers say in frustration – "Bring it here, let me do it." We call that **dysfunctional rescuing** and it is so disempowering. In contrast, Yvonne let me try things, gave me feedback, gave me the space to creatively apply that feedback, and then let me take the glory when I improved. And so I flourished.

I learned so much at Red Cross. Although I didn't know it at the time, **one of the biggest lessons was about how to be an inclusive leader and a good mentor**. Sometimes there is a need to intervene and fight on someone's behalf, and other times you need to let that person fight their own battles in their own way. That delicate balance is the cornerstone of developing talent and creating an inclusive culture; Yvonne was the first person to demonstrate to me what that balance looks like. She also was the first person to fundamentally change my experience of white people. Through knowing her, I realised that you could not lump people together by colour, saying things like, "This is how white people are". Very early in my work life, Yvonne instilled the knowledge in me that I could trust people based on how we related to one another, based on their values rather than on skin colour. She showed me that **what matters is how people make you feel in their presence**.

How I felt in Yvonne's presence was much more meaningful than what she said, although she said a lot. She never saw me as a wounded soldier. She made me see myself as a young social worker joining a team, who was coached where and when needed. At the end of the day, the essence of what she distilled for me was simply that I was equal.

Family ties

DESPITE YVONNE'S EXCELLENT SUPERVISION, after a year I decided it was time to go back home. Also, I was shocked at how little I was earning. I had a lot of people relying on me back home, and honestly had expected to be doing better financially given my post-graduate degree. After my mother's death, our lives changed dramatically. If all went well, my younger brother would soon be starting university, and he would need my financial help.

This brings me to an important point about black family life in South Africa. The **social responsibility** many black people have to large families is so real. The concept of 'nuclear' versus 'extended' family just does not exist for many of us. Even now, I live with my cousin, Johanna, whom I call my sister. What people who don't come from this kind of arrangement fail to understand is that if a cousin or a child of a cousin arrives on your doorstep, that person just assumes you can and will help pay for whatever they are struggling with. Johanna was my emotional pillar of strength after my mom's passing and she practically brought up my two children (and my nephew whom I regard as my child since he came to live with me at the age of four years when his mother died) as if they were her own. That is how we all grew up – if you have a car and a house then you can help others in the extended family. As the person in my family with a university education, I became responsible for dozens of other people.

It is in light of all this that I still remember the amount of that first pay check from Red Cross: R863. "This is not what they said my salary would be", I thought. I had been without parents for many years, and had no understanding of salaries or deductions. Luckily I trusted Yvonne and could ask her about it, which is how I learned about tax and deductions. Even she was surprised by how much I didn't know.

True to form, she explained it in a way that didn't undermine me, saying I wasn't the first to be surprised, and assuring me that other new social workers earned the same amount. This was important to hear, because one of my cousins had suggested I was being cheated. In any case, I knew I needed to earn more, and someone said I could do so if I worked for the private sector as opposed to a government hospital. In addition, I was a young Sowetan through and through, and I yearned to return to Johannesburg. Looking back now on my years at Red Cross, I feel blessed to have had such a positive first work experience.

The danger of labelling

IN JANUARY 1988, I STARTED A NEW JOB at Nicro, an organisation focused on social crime prevention and offender reintegration in Soweto. Having worked with so many abused children at the Burns Unit in Red Cross, I was now tasked with rehabilitating offenders. At Nicro we were supposed to see offenders as people who were hurting, but I was too young and too recently involved with those who had been hurt to handle this extreme contrast. While there, I did learn some important truths about human nature that were helpful to my later work in transformation. Notably, acceptance is the first step to change or rehabilitation.

At our core, every human being wants to be accepted; to matter and belong. People find so many ways to exclude one another. One of the main ways we exclude is by labelling: calling someone a misfit or black sheep, etc. It was at Nicro that I learned **the value of being cautious about labelling people**, an act that is often used as an excuse to dismiss or throw someone away. Instead of labelling, I learned the importance of seeking to understand why a person is in the situation they are in, and how one can help get them out of that situation. Labelling, excluding, and judging people usually digs them in deeper to whatever situation that is causing problems in the first place.

Although I was happy to be back in Johannesburg, it didn't take long for me to see I wouldn't last in this new job. I just didn't have it in me to accept and love people whom I associated with the abusers of the children I had been working with prior to that. Now I understand how a hurting person hurts others, and it is with a little bit of shame that I think about how I reacted back then. But when I got a positive response to a job application I had submitted almost a year ago, I was elated.

Intersectionality in the Free State

WHEN I WAS IN CAPE TOWN contemplating going back to Johannesburg, I had responded to an advertisement in the paper for a number of social work posts at various Eskom power stations. I was now on my way to the Kragbron/Taaibos Power Station in the Free State, where I would be working as an industrial social worker, known at the power station as an 'employee well-being officer'. Part of the Human Resources (HR) team, I was to solve personnel problems among black workers, with a focus on counselling around stress, HIV/AIDs, and alcohol. As was the norm during those days there was a white social worker for the white employees, but despite this segregation, we had equal qualifications and developed a good working relationship.

Once again I was the first African woman with a degree in my work environment; in this case a whole power station. I also had an Honours degree from UCT, which put me in the rare post-graduate category. To add to it, I was young and single. As such, I experienced first-hand the **intersectionality** of being a woman, black, single, and highly educated. In diversity work, intersectionality refers to the ways multi-layered diversity markers can heighten or alter the nature of the discrimination you experience, especially in contrast with someone with whom you share only one diversity marker.

You must **never underestimate the way different dimensions of diversity intersect with each other**. It is easy to say, "We as women experience this", but as a highly educated black woman at that time in South Africa, I experienced a number of other challenges due to the unique combination presented by my gender, race, age, single status and qualifications. For example, if you took a white woman who was also young and single and put her at that power station, she would also experience challenges, but they would differ greatly from mine as a black woman.

In my experience of intersectionality, I have found that race is consistently the strongest ingredient in terms of the outcome of how you are treated and what you experience. This is true in South Africa because of the way racism was institutionalised and so deeply ingrained on a systemic level, with things like the Group Areas Act, etc. This is why I say that race 'colours' most of one's experiences in South Africa. This became especially evident at Kragbron, when management had to figure out the very basic question of where I would live.

As was and is still true in so many parts of South Africa, race determined where you lived and whom you socialised with at the power station. All the black migrant labourers lived in a hostel if they were single, and in black married quarters if they were married. When I arrived, management did not know what to do with me, as I was the only black staff member who didn't fit into either category. I became a subject of board meetings. Finally they decided to give me a big three-bedroom house on my own in the black married quarters. That solution brought its own challenges. The other women were all wives and mostly stay-at-home moms. Being a single, educated woman who related to their husbands from a senior position made them look at me with suspicion. It was such an issue. I tried to develop friendships with them, but it didn't work; I did not 'fit in'. In addition, my work entailed handling some of their private family problems – I just knew too much and I was too different, even though I was part of the same race group.

At the time there were very few women at the power station, and certainly no other black professional women. As a result it was difficult for me to have a social life. I became friendly with the Afrikaans-speaking secretaries and admin staff, but those relationships were limited. Although I knew they meant well, I experienced so many moments of **unconscious bias** when interacting with them. I regularly had to field statements like: "*Julle mense betal nie belasting nie, dit is goed koop om a swart mense te wees want julle eet net pap and morogo*"[11]. Such declarations were invariably followed by the supposedly palliative: "But not you, Nene, you are not like them." Statements like these made me so angry sometimes, but I knew where I was; at times I 'corrected and educated' them, and on other occasions I had to 'choose my battles'. In the end I did not socialise after work. Instead I looked forward to Fridays, when I could drive the 90-minutes home to Soweto, where life felt normal. Every Sunday evening I would drive back to Kragbron, park my car, and be in my big house on my own.

Focus on what you love; Employee Well-Being

DESPITE THE SOCIAL ISOLATION, I loved my job. Originally my focus was on counselling employees on a number of social and family problems including alcohol abuse – sending them to rehabilitation and intervening in cases of abuse with families – but soon I saw that there was so much more that needed to be addressed, especially around HIV prevention, which was still taboo but an exploding problem. As the social worker for all the black workers at the station, I continually came up against the **social consequences of the migrant labour system**, a system responsible for countless broken families and conflicts in South Africa.

I kept seeing the same sad phenomenon. My clients were all men, and most – though not all – had two families; an 'official' wife back at home, and an 'unofficial' wife whom they lived with locally. Some would stay at the

---

[11] "You people do not pay tax and have an affordable lifestyle because you only eat pap and spinach."

power station for years without going home, the only sign of them being husbands and fathers was just sending money to their wives who lived either in the then-homelands or neighbouring countries like Lesotho, Zimbabwe, Mozambique, etc. In addition to the travel costs, one of the main reasons men did not visit home more frequently was the **systemic barrier** of the pass laws and permits in SA at that time. Movement of employees from the homelands into the urban areas was restricted using the notorious Section 10 laws to work and live in what was called 'urban South Africa'[12]. Any African who did not have this permit could not move freely without risk of arrest, so the safest way to limit exposure to that risk – even if you had a valid permit – was to stay put. Over time men in this situation would often find girlfriends or start families closer to their workplace.

As I got more actively involved in the HIV/AIDS space at the power station, I came to realise the role that the dual family system was playing in the spread of the disease. For my preventative trainings to make a real difference, I needed to expand my audience beyond the labourers to include their wives and girlfriends, but I was told that the allocated budget was for employees only. Meanwhile, I would hear my colleagues in HR judging the men for having second wives or girlfriends, saying things like, "That is why AIDS won't stop spreading in this country". Such highly ignorant comments with racist undertones were the order of the day. My frustration grew as I watched the men – many of whom were deeply principled and highly respectable individuals, some as old as my father – being judged and labelled.

The lack of understanding behind those judgements was beautifully captured by the Nigerian novelist, Chimamanda Adichie, in her 2009 TED talk called "The Danger of a Single Story". In it, Adichie talks about the power of story-telling, reminding us of the importance of stories – who tells them, how they are told, and how often they are told. The line that resonates with me is when she talks about how if you tell the story of 'a people' and start with 'secondly', you end up with an entirely different story.

---

[12] The 1948 Group Areas Acts made residential separation of races compulsory, and included legal provisions for where different population groups could own property, reside, and work. A primary goal was to limit the flow of blacks from rural areas into urban and 'whites-only' areas, where economic opportunity was best. The subsequent 1953 Native Laws Amendment Act further narrowed which blacks had the right to permanent residence in towns. Section 10 limited 'urban' residence to blacks born in a town who had lived there continuously for at least 15 years, or blacks continuously employed in a town for the same period.

In the case of the migrant labourers at the power stations, the 'secondly' would be to *start* their story with a tendency to have multiple partners, and then go on to link that tendency to the spread of HIV. In fact, the labourers' stories started *firstly* with the toxicity of the migrant labour system itself; that system's blatant exploitation and disregard for black family structures, and its creation of a social reality that encouraged extramarital partnerships, which in turn often led to second families. Adichie highlighted the importance of starting our stories with their true first principles, because starting a story with 'secondly' invariably obscures a story's full context, resulting in conclusions that fall somewhere between narrow and erratic.

While my white colleagues judged the breakdown of black labourers' families, they saw their own families prioritised. Management went to great lengths to ensure that (white) family structures were preserved. This involved everything from paying relocation allowances, to helping look for schools for children and helping search for employment for wives of white employees – in most cases they would be employed within the same power station. At that time it was not labelled as nepotism, but seen as something positive to encourage families to stay together. So while it is easy to talk about the importance of family, if you are the person whose livelihood requires that you spend almost an entire lifetime away from your spouse and children, the reality is that the temptation to have extramarital partners is huge.

Despite this clear discrepancy in how the system regarded and treated black and white families, my white colleagues looked at the existence of the dual-family system and concluded 'black people are promiscuous'. Meanwhile, my take-away was that apartheid's migrant labour system had for generations destroyed black family structures, and was continuing to do so to that day. My point was not to excuse unacceptable behaviour, but rather to surface hidden dynamics affecting peoples' lives. In other words, it was about **realistically examining the underlying systemic basis for certain behaviours,** because without changing this, it is naïve to expect behaviour to shift. Similarly, when organisations talk about creating a diverse and inclusive workplace, it is important to remember that this work does not only occur at an interpersonal or intrapersonal level; a key part of the shift lies in changing the structural and systemic aspects of exclusion.

Creating an enabling environment

DESPITE JUDGEMENT from some colleagues, I finally got the budget approval to develop preventative programmes around HIV/AIDS for the labourers and their partners. This never would have happened without support from a senior manager at Kragbron who was my line manager's boss.

My line manager and I enjoyed a lukewarm relationship at best. He was white, male, Afrikaans, older, and still busy studying towards the first year of his first university degree, but he was my boss. I was black, female, younger, and had a post-graduate degree from one of the country's best universities. We worked together because we had no choice, but an unspoken awareness that I had greater qualifications permeated our interactions. As a result he tried to undermine me by denying almost every innovative project I proposed.

Fortunately, his boss was a true leader. I'm not sure what his title was, but Tommy Burger was a very senior manager at Kragbron. Like most white people at Eskom, he was Afrikaans. He was in his late 30s, of average build, slightly handsome, very polished and welcoming in his presence. He was also very supportive of me.

One day, Tommy, who believed in the principle of 'management by walking about', noticed me and invited me to present to him on what my job in Employee Well-being was revealing about the power station's culture. In other words, he wanted to know what I thought management needed to be aware of. Reading directly from 10 transparencies (this was the pre-PowerPoint era) jam-packed with my findings on the dual-family system, it was a horrible presentation by today's standards. But Tommy listened patiently. Next to him sat my boss, rolling his eyes, checking his watch, and making sure I could see how disinterested he was.

When I finished, Tommy said, "Wow. Your slides had a lot of text". My boss latched onto that statement and started blabbering negatives, but then Tommy interrupted, "No, no, wait. That's just one minor thing. I really enjoyed it. The content was very good". Until then, management had been totally oblivious to the social repercussions of the dual-family system, and Tommy affirmed the importance of my findings and encouraged me to carry on with that work.

Because of his seniority and positional rank – both in terms of race and gender – Tommy continued to uplift me in ways that I don't think he was even aware of. His patience gave me the confidence to make mistakes and retain my dignity. Because he was senior and showed interest in me, other leaders listened to what I had to say. This is what I mean when I talk about **creating an enabling environment**. It is about wanting people to do better all the time, and knowing how to give people meaningful and constructive feedback so that they can improve without being embarrassed. Tommy commanded a lot of respect from the other senior managers. If you were in his favour, you would never be isolated.

I never called Tommy my mentor but he was just that. He was not 'an Yvonne', but he had an eye for talent, and I sensed my qualifications mattered to him. He could spot potential and wanted to be seen as progressive. **I knew I had an open door with him.** This knowledge – the fact that **we could have a dialogue** – was extremely reassuring to me. One day I was walking from one building to the other and he met me and said, "Do you think people know you enough here in the power station?" I asked what he meant, and he told me that he thought my profile should be raised. Then he said to come see him in his office.

When I met with him, he said that although my home visits with black workers and their families were important, my preventative work had value for everyone – black and white. He pointed out that my individual visits limited me to working with my own race group. He recognised that it was the larger system – where it was unthinkable for a black social worker to provide counselling to white employees – that imposed that limitation, but he wanted to find innovative ways to get beyond that. He suggested profiling me in our internal bulletin so that more people would know about and benefit from the preventative work I was doing.

What was driving him to do that, I still don't know to this day. It was 1988, long before Mandela's release and the changes that would follow, but there were and always will be change agents amongst white people in South Africa.

This is important to remember. Any organisation that takes transformation and sustainable change seriously must always identify allies for change, regardless of race, gender, level, etc.

INSIGHTS & TIPS

One of the greatest lessons I learned during my early years working at the Red Cross Hospital and Kragbron Power Station was the power of leaders to be mentors and to create enabling environments of inclusion.

Understanding Inclusion

Real inclusion means both being and doing

 Practical Tips

- Focusing on the 'being' means regularly asking yourself questions about how people feel in your presence. Do people feel that you are interested in what they are saying? Do people feel accepted and respected? Do they feel they can make mistakes and recover?

- 'Doing' means teaching through action. Do you empower people in your workspace to be able to get on with doing their jobs? For example, at Red Cross Hospital, Yvonne "did" the work of inclusion by actively introducing me to all of the medical heads, by forbidding the other staff members from using me as a translator, and by insisting that I take my turn taking the minutes at staff meetings. Tommy ensured that I was profiled in the newsletter and provided opportunities for me to present my work.

Transformation comes about when leaders authentically live their values

 Practical Tips

- Ask yourself: What are my values? **Am I authentically living these values?**

- If you say you value diversity and inclusion, are you manifesting that in your actions?

The importance of mentors

Look for or be a mentor

 Practical Tips

- Make a meaningful difference in someone's life through engaging and talking openly with them. If you see someone who is dealing with multi-layered complexities (like when I arrived at Red Cross: young, black, new in Cape Town), reach out and lend a hand.

- Accept that everyone, even if they are in a senior position, can benefit from mentoring or coaching. Accept help from another, or open up to somebody and ask him or her to be your mentor.

- Help someone improve their work by offering constructive criticism, but do so without embarrassing them. Find the right moment and also give them credit for what they have done well.

- Ask yourself if your efforts and interactions build or destroy the talents of those around you?

- Remember that mentoring does not always have to be a formal relationship. Tommy was not even my direct boss and never sat down with me and said we had a mentorship relationship, but informally, in his BEING and who he was, he helped to unlock my potential, encouraging me to speak up and grow in confidence.

Know the difference between spoon feeding and mentoring

 Practical Tips

- Guide but never do. This means to give feedback on someone's work by teaching the *principles* of what is needed, but always let the other person do the actual work.

- After giving feedback, give the person space to creatively apply the feedback.

- Let the person take the glory when others give positive feedback - that is development.

Avoid dysfunctional rescuing behaviour

 Practical Tips

- Be aware of dysfunctional rescuing around you. This is when someone's manager intervenes without the person's permission and "rescues" them by doing their job or allocating someone else to do their job while they are still doing it. Instead, always allow a person to do the job themself. If you see problems, offer to coach that person. It will take more time, but ultimately will be better for you both.

Creating an enabling environment and using the power of informal networks.

Great leaders use their rank, power, and privilege to show others the way

 Practical Tips

- Think about how your interest and ability to listen attentively to younger and less experienced employees can aid in their acceptance and development. For example, because Tommy commanded a lot of respect from other senior white managers, his interest in me caused other leaders to listen to what I had to say.

- Do you allow others space and support to make mistakes and to be innovative? The confidence that Tommy built in me allowed me to make mistakes, but to retain my dignity and go on to develop important programmes for the company.

- Do you use your rank and position to give someone access to your informal networks by personally introducing new employees to the leaders in your organisation? In my case, Yvonne personally introduced me to all the medical heads in the hospital, and as a result they knew who I was and that I had a qualification like everyone else.

Know the difference between real inclusion and stereotyping or internalisation

 Practical Tips

- Although having a diverse staff brings many benefits – different points of view, problem-solving approaches, etc. – leaders and managers must ensure that certain staff members are not targeted for their skills that are perceived to "come naturally" based on particular diversity markers.

- For example, being black automatically makes you an interpreter or there are instances where women volunteer to make tea for everyone or to always take minutes in a meeting. While we should always respect the power of choice, we need to also sensitise people to the phenomenon of stereotyping or internalised oppression, where people perpetuate negative stereotypes about their own group. As a leader this means you should always be alert and observant of such behaviour.

- The litmus test is simple in these cases: just ask if a given task is at the level of the person's qualification; do other people also take turns in making tea or taking minutes, or is it always the same person even when they are not employed to do so?

Reach out across race and comfort zones

 Practical Tips

- If you are battling to interact across race groups, rather than just retreating into your comfort zone, look for connection and friendship amongst those who are very different to you.

- Mentorship is not just about sharing technical skills, it is also about understanding the unwritten rules of a different culture that will help you survive better. And when you are not sure what to do? Ask.

- Don't be afraid to ask awkward questions to better understand someone's culture. If you show genuine interest and openness to understanding, people are willing to share.

Don't underestimate the power of structural inequalities

 ## Practical Tips

- So often in corporates we hear people making judgemental statements about others (especially those in townships) for not having family values, but have we looked at and properly understood the system that created this?

- In the workplace, people need to be sensitive to things they do not understand. For example, judging migrant labourers for having two families was a way for management to disregard its responsibility to those families and their well-being. It also removed the focus from a productive, pro-active approach to dealing with what was becoming a serious public health issue, and rather blaming the people involved for their "promiscuity".

- Always question your assumptions before passing judgement – seek to understand the basis for certain behaviours, because without changing the underlying structures, certain behaviour shifts could be impossible.

Awareness of intersectionality

Never underestimate the way different dimensions of diversity intersect with each other

 ## Practical Tips

- It is easy to say, "We as women experience this", but as a woman, I can experience a number of other challenges due to my other diversity markers. As a leader, be careful not to make generalisations about your own or others' experiences.

- In my experience of intersectionality, I have found that race is consistently the strongest ingredient; race tends to colour most of our experience in South Africa. If leaders avoid this fact, it is almost impossible to effect transformation within an organisation.

- Try to understand how intersectionality affects people's performance. For example, when you put all the apparent disadvantages of being black, female and young in the same basket, what unique challenges are presented by that combination?

Chapter 4

RISING TO THE OCCASION

The importance of dialogue (1991)

Where there are experts there will be
no lack of learners.

Swahili Proverb

IN THE EARLY 1990s, ESKOM started 'mothballing', or closing down, certain power stations. Kragbron was among them, and so in 1991 I moved to the nearby Lethabo Power Station.

Lethabo's culture was similar to that at Kragbron. Reflecting the sad norm in South Africa at that time (and to some extent even now), racism was deeply institutionalised, and unfairness glared everywhere. The examples were endless. You could see it in the way supervisors spoke to black people – calling men the 'K-word', saying things like, "You fool, I've given you instructions. Can't you follow instructions?" But it was also present more subtly at the higher levels.

At that time, probably 95% of senior management were Afrikaans speaking. Meetings were always conducted in Afrikaans, and anyone who did not understand had to find a way to catch up. In the beginning, probably 70% of what went on in meetings went over my head. I found it so ironic that back in 1976 the student uprisings had successfully challenged Afrikaans as the medium of instruction in schools, but here I was in 1991, still dealing with it in the workplace.

This example sheds light on how the **minority/majority phenomenon** plays out when you are challenging an issue. The overwhelming number of students who took to Soweto's streets in 1976 had made our goal achievable, but in the corporate environment of 1991, where black professionals were a clear minority, my choice was to assimilate or constantly fight. When I spoke in English people would usually answer in Afrikaans, as if telling me to fall in line, and so I assimilated when it came to language.

Meanwhile, people with lower qualifications continued to be senior to me, and people with the same qualifications earned much more. I remember a white social worker complaining to me about how much was deducted from her salary for tax. When she told me the amount, I did the math. Despite having the same qualifications, I computed that she was on a higher pay 'band'. The only visible difference between us was race. But salary differentials were almost an untouchable subject of discussion, and I continued to sense that I was supposed to feel grateful just to be employed at a professional level.

Raising awareness

DESPITE THE RACISM at Lethabo and within Eskom's general culture, I was thriving professionally. The South African Black Social Workers Association (SABSWA), an external professional body I belonged to which was chaired by a powerful community activist, Anne Letsebe, had nominated me to go for training on HIV/AIDS prevention and education in the USA with the New York State Department of Health. Since SABSWA was paying for all my expenses, Eskom was very supportive in terms of professional development, and approved a five-week study leave that allowed me to go on the trip.

It was my first time abroad, and it was a big deal. I was exposed to a different type of community work, which included joining a mobile night clinic that worked directly with prostitutes in the Bronx and Brooklyn areas, doing pre-HIV test counselling, and providing condoms and other necessities to women who were on the streets. The large numbers of people who came for advice amazed me. It was cutting edge stuff at the time, and with its focus on getting out of the classroom and into the community to deal with real life problems as they presented themselves, it was easily one of the most eye-opening trips I have ever been part of.

When I got back I had so much access to material for my HIV/AIDS programmes that I gathered information and was often invited to speak at conferences, and I started running seminars at Lethabo power station.

For World AIDS Day that year I organised a forum discussion on HIV/AIDS, and managed to secure Dr Reuben Sher as the keynote speaker. Dr Sher was a well-known immunologist who referred to the epidemic as the 'Biological Holocaust' of the time, and went by the moniker 'Mr AIDS', thanks to his pioneering work in tackling the disease head on. I had met him through my association with SABSWA, which again underscored **the importance of the**

networks I was able to access through that and other associations, and how those networks elevated my work.

I told Dr Sher I wanted to run a forum discussion on living with HIV, and to bring in HIV positive people to speak. It was thanks to his suggestion that I made sure to secure a multi-racial panel of HIV-positive people to demonstrate how the disease knows no class or race. My forum included three HIV-positive people: one black woman in her mid-30s, a coloured man in his late 20s, and a white man in his late 30s. I remember the dynamic of that forum so clearly. The hall was packed. The first person to speak was the black woman. She talked about how she had not even been aware there was something called HIV, and only discovered the disease when she presented with symptoms and was then diagnosed.

As she spoke, I looked around the largely white audience, made up mainly of management and technical staff. I could see people were not interested; like it was normal that a black woman would have AIDS. The audience seemed to be waiting to hear from the 'experts' – meaning Dr Sher, who was generally well known (easily recognisable with his signature white beard) and the other white man, who at that point the audience didn't know was also HIV positive.

When the young coloured guy spoke, there was a bit more interest because of how he addressed prejudice. He ruffled feathers by saying, "I know after this, if I drink with that cup", and here he paused to point to the table laid with tea and biscuits for the audience, "many of you would not even want to touch it". There was a lot of discomfort in the room, but he really captured the essence of the overwhelming ignorance of the time.

Then the white guy stood up and said, "My name is so-and-so, and I'm HIV positive". People almost fell off their chairs. Firstly, this man did not look sick or thin, common myths of how all HIV positive people must look at the time, and secondly, he was white. How could a white man have AIDS? Some whispered in the audience. The room went still as he told his story. Dr Sher concluded the day by providing professional scientific and medical information. People were so impressed by what that forum achieved in terms of awareness. There was a buzz for a whole month.

MY EDUCATION PROGRAMMES with the labourers at Lethabo were going well, despite initial resistance from some of the target audience. After all, there I was, 24 years old, telling men – some as old as my father – why it was important to be in monogamous relationships and if they were not, why they must use condoms. They would sometimes look at me like I was speaking another language. Thanks to my earlier findings about the migrant labour system and the dual-family situation that came with it, I knew that teaching men about condoms and prevention was of limited use. Noting their responses during training, I saw the men's likelihood of using condoms was low, so I negotiated with my manager to give me a budget to create a programme on HIV education for female partners.

At first the new education sessions included both men and women, but there was too much discomfort so I decided to run women-only groups. This is where my eyes were opened to how power relations at home influenced public health. The women said, "You must be mad. Do you see me telling this guy to use a condom?" It was in those workshops that I realised you couldn't educate people without empowering them, so I created an assertiveness training programme to empower the women. I got much more information about the challenges they faced when I started talking to the women about more than just condoms and HIV.

For example, learning more about the women's financial situations shed light on the fact that many were fully dependent on the men, and therefore felt they had to succumb to whatever the men wanted (in this case, no condoms). They had little say in the home in general. Slowly I developed a way of working that I continue to use today, that is, creatively adapting the work to what emerges about the system, the context and the people participating in the workshops. The lesson? There is no silver bullet or universal programme that you can use when it comes to human behaviour. You continue to design the programme emergently and remain open to the new understanding that surfaces both for yourself and the participants. Be willing to change and adapt to and include new insights about the system, the context and the participants as the programme unfolds. The work I did on HIV/AIDS education and prevention positioned me to spread my wings wider than just at Eskom. After the session with Dr Sher, he invited me to be a speaker at a national HIV/AIDS conference in Midrand, where I shared my findings and the challenge of the migrant labour system. I recall having a conversation at the conference with a friend, Edwin Cameron, who was the co-founder of the AIDS Consortium and a director of the AIDS Law Project at that time. It was rewarding for me to see that the migrant labour case study I presented captured the interest of people like Edwin, who had already done extensive work in the field of HIV and AIDS. It is amazing how positive feedback encourages us to do more in life.

In the spotlight

WHEREAS MOST OF THE BLACK WOMEN at Lethabo were the ones making tea, I was in the spotlight with my seminars. I often passed by groups of employees on my way to or from another office or building. They would be sitting together taking their lunch break outside in the shade, and Yoh! - the whistles and shouting that sometimes came! "*Ntombenhle, dhudlu*"[13] they'd say. One day I passed these workers while walking with a white colleague – she was practically traumatised by the experience. She couldn't understand how I could be so cool about it, and said I was encouraging the behaviour by not responding.

It was true that under normal circumstances what those men were doing could be an immediate case to take to the Industrial Relations (IR) department for sexual harassment. It took me a while to think of the most appropriate way to address this. Even though I did not grow up in that particular culture where appreciation was expressed in that way, I had read or heard stories that there are some people who do that. Reflecting on the situation, I considered how in many other settings within the power station the same men respected me for the professional role I played in their lives. I found the first entry point of addressing this when they came to my office individually for various consultations. I recall an instance when one of the 'whistlers' came to my office about a personal issue. He didn't understand why this was an issue, explaining to me that the comments were appreciation and acknowledgement of a beautiful woman. I actually believed that he didn't mean any disrespect – it was how he had been socialised growing up – so in that situation I realised I had a choice to be a victim or an educator.

---

[13] "Beautiful woman, big woman"

My response was to add sexual harassment and gender-relations education as a subject in my prevention seminars. Just like that, a workshop was developed. In these sessions, a lot of the men echoed the whistler's sentiment that they didn't understand why their compliments would offend women. Some said the problem was that those of us who grew up in urban areas like myself had adopted 'white culture'. I planned a session and asked the power station manager to speak from his point of view as a man (versus taking a legal perspective). He listened to the men (through translation) and said, "If this is your culture that is fine, but you just can't do it here". And that actually helped; at the time people listened to authority. In addition, there were other younger black men who participated in these sessions and agreed with my explanation.

What emerged in these sessions was the importance of dialogue. When you recognise how cultural nuances are influencing a situation, you can't just get angry and take people to IR. In short, by making an effort to understand that people's worldviews are different, we got better results than we would have by taking the legal route. Slowly, through dialogue, I educated people from the black male labourers to the white female secretaries. I wasn't consciously doing diversity work then, but in a way those sessions were where this work began for me.

Shocking treatment at the Power Station Clinic

IN MOST ESKOM POWER STATIONS, Employee Well-being Officers (social workers and psychologists) worked out of the medical centres, and I was given a beautiful office right near the clinic. When I started at Lethabo there were no senior black nurses, only black nursing assistants, so people were not used to black professional women in that space. I often used a company car (then called a pool car) – a white Toyota Corolla – to do my home visits in the nearby township of Sebokeng, where half of the black staff and their families lived (the other half being in the hostel). Every time I would leave the main gate driving that car, the security guards would tell me, "You make us so proud". A black woman driving a pool car was still a rarity there, and it made me happy to be able to model that for them.

From my office in the medical centre I clearly observed discrimination in multiple forms. Early on I had heard stories from black patients who told me they were given weak medications – like Panado or paracetamol – regardless of what their problem was, compared to whites who received stronger medications (e.g. antibiotics or whatever was medically required). I actually thought it was folklore until sometime later when I asked two black nursing assistants and they confirmed it was true. It frustrated them as well, but there was little they could do since they had to get permission from the white senior nurse to distribute medications.

Even when supervisors themselves brought black people to the clinic – in cases where workers were seriously injured – there was so much drama and distrust. The supervisors would be shouting at the injured workers, and the sisters would side with the supervisors without even hearing the workers' stories. I would see these things but couldn't intervene because I wasn't a nursing sister and had no way of analysing the true state of someone's medical condition. But what I could see was that black workers were always viewed as trying to dodge work, whereas when a white worker came in, everything stopped. White people's pain was taken so seriously.

I remember an older man who came into the clinic. I think he had injured his hand – he was in a lot of pain. As usual, the nurse was asking why he was trying to avoid work, telling him he was lying and lazy. The way the nursing sister was disrespecting this man old enough to be my father, seeing him going through that kind of pain, but also seeing the anger than he could not express – it made me so embarrassed to witness his pain on all those different levels. And because of African culture, where age is so respected, when his eyes met mine I felt hurt myself, seeing his embarrassment.

I decided to call him to my office. He came in and there were almost tears in his eyes as he tried to explain what had happened. Suddenly his boss barged into my office. "Here you are gallivanting again. What story are you cooking up now?", he shouted, without even acknowledging me. I intervened, saying I was the one who had called the man to my office. "Anything to do with a black person talking to a black person has to be dodgy in your view?" I said, challenging him. To my utter surprise he said, "Yes". I was so shocked that for a moment I just kept quiet. I must be honest that my silence was more an attempt to stop my voice from shaking than it was a lack of words. My head was stuck on the 'women are emotional' narrative that I had to avoid confirming to this man. After a few moments I managed to ask him to excuse us and leave, as we were still busy talking. "Not without this loafer", he replied. When the gentlemen stood up and apologised in Sesotho for causing trouble for me with 'the whites', I had to hold back my tears again. Here he was seeing me as a daughter, now feeling sorry for what he perceived as trouble coming my way. I escalated the incident to senior management and some meetings took place, but nothing serious ever happened to that supervisor.

Organisations are a microcosm of the larger society

IF THINGS WERE NOT GREAT inside the station, outside the power station in Vereeniging town, the racism was even worse. There was an evening when an old friend from Soweto was visiting me. It was late and the township shops had closed, so we had gone to a take-away shop in the city centre. I left her in the car while I went in, ordered and paid at a counter, and then sat down to wait in a chair. The shop owner said, "No, you can't wait here. Go sit in your car", waving me away. I left the shop, humiliated. It all happened so quickly. I didn't tell my friend what had happened, and acted like I was just coming to wait with her, but I was going through this intense inner turmoil. I had already given the shop owner my money, and was furious with myself for not insisting that he give it back. And now here I was, actually waiting. I hated myself for allowing myself to be discriminated against like that. I felt so defeated. I never did tell my friend what had happened.

I recount that episode in order to bring up an important point about transformation work. Sometimes you chastise yourself for not standing up for yourself. Other times you chastise yourself for speaking up, but having come across clumsily. Personally I find that I am constantly aware of fighting the 'angry black woman' narrative. However you decide to respond, dealing with racist events is a daily dance of emotions, and striking a healthy balance between your emotions and how you handle such incidents is easier said than done.

In the case of the take-away in Vereeniging, the offender already had my money. Whether I chose to walk away or fight he would still have my money, so from his perspective, he won either way. This is by no means a call for people to shove things under the carpet, but what it demonstrates is that on any given day you have so many things to deal with, and **sometimes**

the right choice is to take care of your own heart. Ignoring a situation may communicate to others that you are not standing up for yourself, but those others don't know what you have already been through on the same day, or what your own decision process is. **It is all about your own inner work**. This applies to the workplace as well. It is important not to judge someone who chooses not to fight when racism or discrimination occurs.

Towards the end of my time at Lethabo I felt I had become the social worker for everything. There was too much expectation on me to be the saviour for all the black workers there. I was constantly trying to help them in what they went through with their supervisors, their spouses, and their children; all with the unfairness and the inconsistent application of HR policies and systems. I see now that my transformation efforts were mostly happening at an inter-personal level, and it was wearing me out.

Transformation fatigue comes from constantly fighting inter-personal battles, but it can also come from fighting or challenging the system without the necessary support. Ultimately a systemic response at an organisation-wide level is required. That means a response that questions the structures, policies, procedures, and practices that are the norm in an organisation. Deep reflection and committed action is required at the leadership level around all the elements of the organisational system and how these may or may not be mitigating transformation efforts either consciously or unconsciously. Whether in society or in organisations, transformation and culture change cannot rely only on a few individuals.

INSIGHTS & TIPS

As my time at Eskom progressed, I started to develop a way of working that I continue to use today, that is, creatively adapting to what emerges in the course of assessing employee needs, designing interventions and workshops through close observation, and constant questioning of inter-personal and organisational dynamics.

There is no 'one-size-fits-all' approach to transformation

Be willing to customise, align, and incorporate the nuances of every situation

 Practical Tips

- You may think that you have a suitable training programme that addresses important issues, but let your audiences also be your teachers.

- Always allow your own assumptions as a trainer or facilitator to be challenged.

You cannot educate without empowering

 ### Practical Tips

- Create a space for open dialogue that can go beyond the immediate subject that you want to educate people about. Find out who people are, and allow them to share and learn from one another.

- Remember that all the education in the world will not help if people are not empowered to act on it.

The importance of continual professional development

Ensure that professional development opportunities are fairly distributed and make the most of professional networks/associations

 ### Practical Tips

- Making sure that all of your top performers have access to professional development opportunities (across race, gender and other diversity markers) is key to a level playing field when it comes to performance.

- Encourage yourself and your employees to play an active role in professional networks and associations. Particularly for people from disadvantaged groups, it can make such a difference to have the support and help of professional associations and groups that understand where you are coming from.

Open dialogue to understand cultural differences

Education will be longer and more tedious than legal routes, but it is worth it

 ### Practical Tips

- You cannot assume that people will 'get it' the first time. Be prepared and willing to commit time to real dialogue and everyone will benefit.

- Be sure everyone is on the same page when you are defining something that can be subjective and/or cultural (e.g. to some people sexual harassment means rape, touching, etc., while to others, comments are already too much).

- After education sessions, assess whether there is a change in the problematic behaviour. If nothing has changed, you are dealing with a different story and may need to try a different intervention.

Leaders must lead to ensure the adoption of policies and inclusive practices in their organisations

 Practical Tips

- When there is a clear issue around language policy or when employees feel they are being excluded because of language, leaders and senior managers need to be responsive and decisive in enforcing the use of the official (most inclusive) language.

- When language issues are raised, your position as a leader requires role modelling, inclusiveness, and decisiveness. Confront such situations with sensitivity and lead by example.

- Find creative ways to extend the learning that you get in your organisation to the broader society, especially those around us like family and friends.

- Challenge sexist, racist and homophobic statements, or any statements or behaviours that denigrate other people. This will make you a change catalyst within your circles of influence.

Handling transformation fatigue

Take care of your heart

 Practical Tips

- Be aware that on any given day you may have many instances of prejudice or discrimination to deal with, and sometimes the right choice is to take care of your own heart.

- Do not judge someone who chooses not to fight when racism or discrimination occurs. You do not know how many other battles he or she had to fight earlier on.

- Timing is key. When you are on the receiving end of discrimination, you have a choice to either confront it immediately or take time to reflect on the timing and impact of your response. Always give yourself time to take ownership of your reaction to situations that you cannot control.

Transformation cannot rely only on a few individuals: systemic change is needed

Stop trying to save everyone all the time

 Practical Tips

- Remember that transformation and building an inclusive culture in society or in organisations cannot rely only on a few individuals.

- Look for transformation allies and build networks of support; constantly fighting inter-personal battles is totally unsustainable.

- Fighting or challenging the system without the necessary support is also self-defeating.

- A systemic response at an organisation-wide level is required for real change to come about. This means a response that questions the structures, policies, procedures, and practices that are the norm in an organisation.

Chapter 5

LEVELLING THE PLAYING FIELD

Defining employment equity (1992-95)

Everyone has the right to have red eyes, blue eyes
or brown eyes. Everyone has a right to be different,
particularly if the distinguishing features are immutable.

Dikgang Moseneke
Former Deputy Chief Justice of South Africa

THE DESIRE TO RETURN to Johannesburg never left me, and when a
vacancy opened at Eskom's headquarters at Megawatt Park, I seized the
opportunity. Not only did this job bring me home, it also was a promotion
within an exciting new department: Senior Advisor in the Department of
Social Harmonisation. Social Harmonisation was the department charged
with implementing Eskom's new employment equity and affirmative action
policies.

It was 1992 and things were changing fast, especially at HQ. Eskom's senior
management saw that a new government would be coming out of the engine
room soon enough; they wanted us to start changing ourselves before
government came and did it for us. Eskom was one of the few organisations
that started transformation before any legislation was promulgated, and now
I was going to be part of the team making this happen.

Returning to Johannesburg was a homecoming to normalcy. I lived in a block
of company flats in Sunninghill, close to Megawatt Park. It was such a relief
to be in a place where I could be one of many. My new work environment
was also liberating. I was finally in an office where black professionals were
not unusual, such as my new boss, Dawn Mokhobo. In addition, I had moved
out of social work and into Human Resources, and my new position allowed
me to work with everyone; there was no longer the limitation of dealing with
white or black people only.

Leadership had identified various steps to transformation, including the
need to 'harmonise' the environment, or create an atmosphere conducive
to change. My portfolio was primarily focused on preparing staff at all levels
to be part of this new environment. In addition to organising and running
workshops and trainings, I also put support structures in place. For example,

if a power station wanted to establish an employment equity committee, I would figure out what training best supported the committee in that particular power station, and then organise it. Thanks to my social work background I had a broad range of skills to draw on, from facilitation to training, and I moved between all the stations, helping to set up the needed structures.

Correcting the imbalances

BUT WHAT WAS EMPLOYMENT EQUITY, and how did you create it? I would try to explain to people that a big part of employment equity at that stage was about **levelling the playing field through affirmative action**. When we talk about levelling the playing field, we first have to acknowledge that the field was made unequal by the apartheid government. **Affirmative action was about correcting those imbalances**. To use myself as an example: I got to Kragbron, I already had a degree, and there was no question about my qualifications, so affirmative action was not saying I must be promoted unfairly; what it was saying was that my boss should not have lower qualifications than me while people talked about merit. In other words, affirmative action was meant to identify and correct anomalies like this by putting black people where they deserved to be, but were not because of past misalignments.

I was constantly at pains to explain the difference between proper affirmative action and tokenism. **Affirmative action was never meant to be tokenism**. There was a lot of push back from both whites and blacks on the concept of affirmative action because of how it was labelled and stigmatised. Whites would mock it, calling people 'affirmative action appointees', as if there was something faulty with them. And because we grew up in an era where blacks were called so many things – Bantus, other-than-white, non-white, etc. – being labelled in this new way triggered historical pain, so black people also pushed back. A lot of people didn't want to be called affirmative action appointees, saying, "I got here on merit". **The perception that merit and affirmative action were somehow mutually exclusive became a powerful narrative that we still battle today**. But affirmative action was never meant to be about bypassing merit; rather it was about equalising the recognition of merit, and ensuring equal opportunities to perform.

I remember one black engineer who was very vocal in his rejection of affirmative action. He said, "I'm an engineer, I'm qualified, I don't need a special programme". He was in his department for less than seven months when a white colleague who had started around the same time got his second promotion. That's when he started questioning the system. When his case came to me I didn't miss an opportunity to say I told you so. Now he understood the painful reality, which was that **affirmative action was not about saying there is something wrong with you, but rather acknowledging that there was something wrong in the system**.

So we tried to fight it. His department said, "No, no, the white engineer is performing better". The black engineer said, "We started the same week, how much better can his performance be?" When we dug deeper, we found the white engineer was being mentored, given exposure to more projects, going to seminars, having his hand held. So yes, he was more advanced after seven months, but he was also receiving exposure to all these things that the black engineer was not. So this is what I mean by equal opportunity to perform. There was so much going on under the surface, and the transformation agenda finally gave us a platform to start naming and exposing these dynamics.

Naming the narratives

I STARTED TO RUN what we called "**anti-racism workshops**". They were the first of their kind at Eskom; they were very good and at times very controversial. A lot of things were unravelled in those workshops. We didn't have the language of unconscious bias back then, so it was the first time we were exposing what was happening both above and below the surface – issues like discrimination in managing performance and pay scales; the message that was sent by keeping amenities separate; the lack of respect paid to black managers in the way white managers spoke to them; and the way subordinates did not listen to black managers but jumped at an instruction from a white person, even if that person was below the black manager. Many people attended these workshops, which normally accommodated about 30 participants who were mixed across colour lines but came from similar professional bands.

The need for these workshops – which meant to expose conscious and unconscious racism – became apparent literally from the moment they began. One of the first exercises we did was to ask everyone to write down their given names. In those days black people rarely used their proper African names at work because of the perception that it was too difficult for white people to pronounce them. "Just call me 'Tom'", they would say. After everyone had written their names down, we would ask them to change what was on their nametags and replace whatever they had written. Most of the black people had to cross out what they had written and replace it with their given names.

Some white participants handled this exercise well, but others struggled. "I'm used to calling you John, and suddenly you are Nhlanhla? – I cannot even pronounce that name. I look at you and I see John. What's the big deal, this is what we have been calling you anyway". There was less sensitivity in those days, but processes like these allowed people to identify all kinds of triggers and slights, big and small. Things that speak to upbringing: the stereotypes and narratives we pick up and perpetuate without ever asking why.

One of my triggers – even now it remains a passionate subject for me – is when people refer to a person using a negative term, for example calling me 'non-white'. This term basically uses whiteness as a yardstick. Why refer to me by starting with someone else? We would have hot arguments about this in our workshops. Eventually I would point to a man, and say, "If I were to call you a non-woman, you would ask me why I'm calling you that, wouldn't you? So you cannot negate my being by referring to me in negative terms". Of course people understood when I explained it that way.

What I wanted them to see was that calling a black person a 'non-white' is a subtle way of saying that whiteness is superior and that everything starts with whites. I actually met one of my workshop participants years later who said that that lesson had a huge impact on him. He remembered me asking, "Why do you negate my being by using yourself as a yardstick?", and something clicked for him. He realised he had just grown up saying this without questioning its merits. And that was exactly the point: in South Africa we have such a long history of calling black people by so many names other than the ones of their choosing.

So those were the types of things we spent time unpacking and explaining. The workshops brought out a lot of the biases that operated below the surface. Sometimes it was painful for people, but it was so important because **without naming the narratives you cannot hope to change them**. I'd like to say that this has all changed, but it is amazing how often I still address so many of the same issues today. Looking back at my journey and the workshops I facilitated, an interesting observation is that most of the dialogues centred on issues of race and gender. This is quite understandable given the period covered. Whenever issues of age, sexual orientation, religion etc. came to the fore, the discussion would always revert back to race and gender. Although the skills of addressing these are applicable across all dimensions of diversity, there is more of a pull now to look at diversity comprehensively and ensure that prejudice does not migrate from one dimension to another. For example, it would be hypocritical to be passionate about eradicating racism, and yet be casual about the hatred and violence that is often directed at people who do not subscribe to hetero-normative rules of society.

Structural Overhauls

WHILE WE WERE BUSY QUESTIONING THE NARRATIVES that infused the daily interactions, Eskom's CEO was digging deep to shift the racial dynamics operating at the organisation's top levels. A visionary leader with a bold presence and bushy eyebrows over a warm face, Dr Ian McRae was one of the leaders who made an effort to effect change. Not to say he didn't make mistakes, but his leadership allowed us to co-create a truly progressive diversity and transformation programme. Ian showed everyone how leadership can create space for transformation and how change is driven from the top.

Thanks to Ian's leadership, Eskom not only had a **succession plan** years before the government required Employment Equity, but it also enacted its succession planning at the highest levels to pave the way for transformation. As CEO, Ian sat at the top of Eskom's leadership hierarchy. Under the CEO were the executive directors, all of whom were white men. To address this imbalance, Ian created a new layer of senior general managers (SGMs) who were understudies to those executive directors, and all were black.

The SGMs were mentored with a clear objective of taking over from the white executive directors. This was real **space creation**, and I credit Ian's leadership for the way succession planning unfolded with so little friction at Eskom. The succession plan changed Eskom, and a lot of companies looked to us as an example of how to do similar things in their organisations in the years that followed.

Eskom also started an **accelerated development programme**, led by my friend Sebina Hlapolosa – an eloquent, passionate and beautiful woman full of energy and drive. Accelerated development was about offering mentorship and training to speed up the process of preparing qualified black professionals for leadership positions. Within Eskom, it was a formal programme exposing participants to different leadership challenges. One interesting component was the focus on '**rough edges**'. It addressed the fact that young professionals were coming into the workplace but lacked important knowledge about the world of work. It was behavioural stuff that as a person in a leadership position you would be expected to know. For example, the importance of speaking up, of being assertive and putting your point across in a convincing manner.

The training also included subtle things, like how to behave at a business dinner. As much as some people criticised this training, accusing us of trying to make people white, the point was that if you grew up in a home where no one had ever been to a formal dinner party where you sit around a table, how could you expect to know the rules that pertained? Even if some people felt like it was demeaning to have these things pointed out, it was more embarrassing to go to a dinner and be the only one who did not know how to use the appropriate glasses or cutlery. These days we would never run that kind of training. There's not as much of a need, as information is more generally available now through the Internet etc.

ANOTHER FORMALISED SUPPORT at Eskom was the **Black Consultative Forum (BCF)**, which we created in 1994. The BCF was a **support group for black professionals** to build ourselves personally and collectively, and to discuss challenges of race and gender in an accepting space. As secretary of the BCF, whenever a new black professional joined Eskom, I would reach out and encourage that person to join. It was voluntary, but the majority actively took part. The BCF was helpful for so many reasons.

Despite its transformation efforts, Eskom was still known as an Afrikaans organisation and had only recently started to install black managers. Ian's work with people at the top was ground-breaking, but changes in the middle came more slowly and we still faced a lot of resistance. The BCF gave us a strong voice to challenge management when we saw things requiring change. For example, if in a department black people were consistently receiving lower ratings in performance reviews and whites were always rated highly, we could investigate what was really going on. The BCF was very active in those days, and we often went for break-aways, even over weekends, to strategise, host seminars, etc. To its credit, Eskom supported us by covering accommodation and other costs for those break-aways.

The BCF also served as a safe space to deal internally with things about which we felt we needed to be particularly vigilant. Because there was already so much criticism around one's blackness, a lot of us felt it was important to actively ensure we didn't feed certain narratives (e.g. 'black people are always late'). It didn't matter if you were an engineer, accountant, or marketing specialist – you may have your qualifications but your blackness remained a disadvantage, so we identified for each other ways to minimise that negative spotlight.

The BCF also had a direct channel to the CEO. Whenever a promotion opportunity arose, Ian asked us to recommend candidates, and took our candidates seriously. In fact, Ian eventually asked the BCF to identify a successor for himself. He also would come and listen to us whenever there were hot issues playing out, for example, a black person not being given exposure or support in his department. Even on a Saturday Ian would show up, and if he couldn't come himself, he would delegate someone from HR.

I was not in a senior position in those days and so had little direct contact with Ian, but I remember a weekend when just a few of us from the BCF met with him. There had been some noise in the organisation questioning why the BCF was necessary, and so we had come together that weekend – with Ian – to define our objective as a group. I was struck by Ian's listening skills and clear desire to understand our needs. I have talked about the importance of how a person makes you feel in his presence. In Ian's presence, I felt confident and respected. I felt I could be myself. **He was not a person who was interested in intimidating anyone. His focus was always on**

understanding what was being said. I thought all CEOs were like that – I only discovered later that Ian's attitude was not the norm.

Personal Development

THANKS TO THE SUPPORT AND COMMITMENT OF MY HR EXECUTIVE, BONGANI KHUMALO, to developing people, I was able to attend numerous conferences and made additional trips to the USA to improve my knowledge and skills in diversity work. One of my big take-aways from those trips to the USA was that what we were battling in South Africa, America was also still battling. I also learned so much about how to have productive dialogues in which people could truly express themselves.

Those trips further broadened my understanding of diversity beyond race and gender, to include age, country of origin, sexual orientation, disability, marital status, etc., and taught me the importance of unlearning terms like 'tolerance', whose negative connotations poisoned diversity work in its early years. Diversity – blackness, femaleness, etc. – were not qualities to be 'tolerated', but rather were attributes to be acknowledged and embraced.

As my knowledge and experience in diversity work deepened, so did my perceptions. I started to notice a tendency in some black people to emphasise race at the expense of other aspects of diversity, and how this problematic dynamic revealed self-interest more than it did a desire to fight for what was right and fair. Having said that, the concept of intersectionality must once again be mentioned here, as it shows how **diversity markers exist in a pecking order**, where race tends to dominate one's experiences because of how it is tied to structural and systemic inequalities. In South Africa, because apartheid policies functioned on a racial basis, race remains by far the strongest determinant of deep injustice. Nonetheless, it was vital to recognise that race was not everything; we needed to become equally passionate about fighting sexism, ageism, and other inequalities.

MEANWHILE, I HAD ALSO COME TO NOTICE the existence of certain black executives – usually people who had 'made it' – who didn't want to hear anything about race or transformation, regardless of whom it was for. I particularly remember one manager who always said he only wanted to talk 'core business', as if talk of transformation must be to the exclusion of 'business'. This manager felt no personal responsibility to advance transformation goals, and his attitude clearly expressed the belief that a focus on transformation was a type of weakness.

Some people said I saw colour in everything which did make me question myself, but ultimately I realised that this 'just because I'm black doesn't mean I need to talk about transformation' attitude was another form of internalisation of negative messages. It frustrated me deeply. I have seen black executives deliberately talking down to other black people, joining in jokes that were self-denigrating just to be seen to be 'above' race issues.

For me, this type of attitude and behaviour does us a great disservice. As a senior person, you actually have the power to exert influence and be taken seriously, to educate your colleagues and subordinates about things that might not be obvious. For someone who is confident in his or her role, why not also be an agent of change?

NOW IT WAS 1994, and I was part of the **CEO's Programme**, a prestigious track for employees who showed potential as leaders. You had to be nominated by your direct supervisor to take part, and blacks were always a minority. We were in a leadership seminar and had spent the day examining case studies on change, lack of change, the core business at Eskom – multiple topics of concern to leadership.

We were discussing the recent policy change that established English as the official language at Eskom (previously there had been a dual-language policy) and a fierce debate was sparked. I spoke up, saying how managers who continued to insist on speaking Afrikaans in meetings not only disadvantaged people who did not understand the language, but also perpetuated a larger culture of exclusion. An Afrikaans woman argued with me and insisted, "Why do people have a problem with my Afrikaans language?" I explained that we were all making accommodations, that English was also not my first language. "I speak Setswana and I am already meeting you halfway by speaking English, so you need to do the same", but she refused to see the point, and genuinely thought too much was being asked of Afrikaans people. I was shocked by her ignorance. Even worse was that despite now being reminded that English was also not the first language of most black people, she was still so unwilling to appreciate how black people had walked the other side of reconciliation for such a long time.

This debate resonated at a deeper level because by sheer coincidence it happened to take place on the day of Mandela and FW De Klerk's pre-election debate which was facilitated by Freek Robinson of the SABC. It was an intense debate about South Africa's future stability and why things had to change. Watching it together as the delegates of the CEO's Programme, we were literally divided into black and white. All the black people thought Mandela had won the debate and the white participants thought FW de Klerk had won. You must remember that Mandela was not yet popular among white people, who were relating totally differently to him back then. I can say that the mood in the room captured that of South Africa at the time: whites fearing and resisting change, and blacks increasingly impatient for the change that must come *now*.

Leading up to the elections terrible violence had been flaring in different parts of the country. People were dying and we all had our worries. One of the first questions in the debate was about that violence – something about what guarantee there was that the violence wouldn't get out of control. I remember white people in the group saying, "The violence is happening in your townships, how do you blame our president for your violence?" Meanwhile we were saying that the violence was happening because of a lack of change. Then they would say, "But you are the guys fighting, so why blame it on us?" So we got into that fierce argument of: "Your this, our that", and it took us nowhere. The discussion was heated, we argued back and forth, emotions all over the place. Finally the facilitator had to end it. We agreed to disagree but we all knew what was coming, and you could feel the tension.

INSIGHTS & TIPS

One thing that became very clear to me in this time was that in any transformation forum or initiative, the CEO's visible supportive can make or break your efforts.

Strong leadership drives transformation

Leadership must drive transformation

 Practical Tips

- Remember that when leaders drive transformation from the top it gives the whole exercise credibility, which filters through the organisation. This must be the starting point for any effective and sustainable transformation programme.

- Leaders must continually show their support in both their being – how they make people feel in their presence, and their doing – their actions (e.g. the creation of a succession plan and their availability to engage with issues of diversity and to make appropriate changes).

- Leaders must be ready for the discomfort this process can bring. Where leaders do this authentically, the benefits are enormous and visible.

Addressing and breaking the narratives

One of the most critical parts of breaking the cycle of racism is addressing the stereotypes and narratives that persist and perpetuate prejudice and discrimination.

Be part of openly naming and challenging narratives

 Practical Tips

- Organisations must open their systemic baggage and collectively confront what is in there. The narratives circulating around an organisation need to be named and exposed for what they are.

- Triggers and slights, big and small, should be raised openly so people are aware of them.

- My pastor likes to say "The power of sin is in its secrecy". If you don't talk about things, they remain embedded in the corridors. Talking about things begins to take away their power.

- Ask yourself and your leadership team whether you have found yourselves expressing any of the following common negative narratives about transformation:

  ○ "Hiring black people mean lowering standards."

  ○ "Our organisation is a meritocracy, we only appoint (women/ blacks) if they are qualified, etc."

  ○ "Merit is the sole preserve of white people."

  ○ "Black appointments and merit are mutually exclusive."

  ○ "Employment equity will mean there are no opportunities for whites."

The importance of good facilitation

 Practical Tips

- Having a facilitator who can frame things productively – meaning clearly, logically and calmly – is key to productive dialogue.

- A good facilitator must be able to unpack people's comments, never get upset, and never get personally entangled in the dialogue.

- Use a good facilitator who models inclusivity in seeing, listening for and inviting all views and perspectives.

Don't let others define Employment Equity for you

Don't be ashamed to be a product of Employment Equity

 Practical Tips

- Remember that acknowledging that you got to where you are because of Employment Equity doesn't change who you are or the value, competency or qualifications that you bring.

- Acknowledging the value of EE only proves that there were, and still are, artificial barriers that prevent equal access for some people.

- Be aware of the danger of confusing what is a legitimate strategy with so-called "window dressing".

- There is only shame in EE when you let others define what it is.

Understanding affirmative action

Untangling affirmative action, merit and performance

 Practical Tips

- To understand affirmative action, you must first acknowledge that the playing field is not level, due to historical and systemic imbalances.

- The second step is to accept that affirmative action is a legitimate strategy that is meant to correct the imbalances of the past by removing artificial barriers that prevent access to some people. Just because affirmative action has its critics does not invalidate its principles. It is important to remember that affirmative action was never meant to be about bypassing merit – rather it was about equalising the recognition of merit and ensuring equal opportunities to perform.

- The third step is to acknowledge that affirmative action is one way to act inclusively. Organisations have to *do* something to rectify the imbalances of the past, because it won't happen naturally on its own.

Equal opportunity and performance

Practical Tips

- Be aware when discussions about affirmative action and merit often lead to a manager citing "better performance" as the reason why a white person is being promoted over a black person.

- In these situations, dig deeper and ask if candidates are receiving equal exposure to things like mentorship, interesting projects, seminars and professional development. That is, are the candidates being given equal opportunity to perform?

Creating structural change

Do succession planning right

Practical Tips

- Good succession planning requires visible action and support from the leadership.

- Transformation should happen at all levels, from the very senior to the lowest levels.

- People must be mentored properly and given time to learn the ropes.

- Promises made about succession planning should be taken to their correct end.

Create leadership programmes

Practical Tips

- Have a leadership programme that is not all black, but that targets certain black people to accelerate their development and ensures that the learning (for everyone) happens in a diverse environment.

- Distinguish between a leadership programme and a special interest group.

Communication around all interventions must be clear

 Practical Tips

- Provide clear communication that unravels the complexity around employment equity and affirmative action measures, and how they will be implemented in your organisation.

- Clearly communicate the motivation and goals of all interventions and make sure these are understood at all levels (from leadership to the lowest levels).

Support the support groups

 Practical Tips

- Initiate support groups where professionals from previously disadvantaged groups can discuss personal and collective professional challenges and find innovative solutions in the professional space.

- Use these groups to discuss problems, analyse priorities, and have a collective voice to bring challenges to management.

- Ensure that support groups have a direct line to senior leadership.

- Use such groups as a safe space to offer feedback within the group about your own behaviour, in order to prevent actions that are counter-productive to being seen and treated equally.

Deepening our understanding of diversity and counter-productive fears

Fighting internalised oppression and stereotype threats

 Practical Tips

- Remember that diversity work can trigger different things for different people, including people from disadvantaged groups who may actively fight efforts to challenge the system. The only way to handle this is through respectful communication, i.e. listening to people and valuing their opinions.

- Especially with senior people, remind them that they are best positioned to exert influence and be taken seriously when it comes to educating their colleagues and subordinates about things that might not be obvious.

- If you are feeling a stereotype threat, remember that you are bigger than the stereotypes that people would apply to you. Rise above them.

- Remember that when change is required in a system, burying your head in the sand or saying, "I only mind my own business" is not demonstrating the qualities of a good change agent.

Recognise the effects of fear

 Practical Tips

- Be aware that fear exerts a heavy and negative influence on how people behave, what they are willing to risk, and how open they can make themselves.

- Remember that the Nelson Mandela whom whites so feared back in 1994 became their hero too. His gesture of reconciliation, which a number of black people felt was overextended without reciprocity, shows how patience, forgiveness, and tolerance are fundamental to transformation.

- In the corporate context, reciprocity and authentic effort on the part of management are critical ingredients to transformation; without these, transformation efforts will likely consist mostly of false starts and lip service.

Chapter 6

LEADING FROM THE FRONT

Multiplying Equity (1995-1997)

A good chief is like a strong tree with many branches, people like to sit in its shade.

South African Proverb

DEMOCRACY CAME TO SOUTH AFRICA in April 1994. Nelson Mandela was president, and for the first time in its history, our country functioned according to the one person-one vote principle. The competing dynamics of fear and expectation that had been playing out for months were still very present, with many white people anxious about where they would end up, and most black people consumed by heightened expectations. As black people were in the majority, the overwhelming feeling was a palpable sense of hope: exiles were coming home, and South Africa was abuzz with the excitement of the unknown.

It was one thing to win the elections and finally have a democratically elected government, but quite another to put the systems in place to realise the dream of an equal and just society. The task before us was unprecedented. Although transformation in every sector was vital, removing the gross inequalities that kept black people in economic shackles was seen as a clear prerequisite to liberating other aspects of our lives. The democratisation of labour and the workplace was also seen as an area where legislative changes could have an immediate impact. In May 1994, President Mandela appointed Tito Mboweni as Minister to the Department of Labour (he later became Reserve Bank Governor), which was tasked with nothing less than creating the legislative basis for transforming a labour market previously defined by the codified discrimination and injustice of apartheid's laws.

During this exciting time in South Africa's transformation, Sebina Hlapolosa, who was the head of the accelerated development programme, called me in to say that the Department of Labour (DoL) was looking for good people, and would I be interested? Thrilled at the prospect, I went for an interview with Sipho Pityana, the Department's new Director General (DG). I walked out of that interview struck by the DG's obvious passion for his work and charged with excitement at the idea of being directly involved with the team shaping the future of South Africa's labour market. Because the DoL couldn't match the salary I was earning, Eskom seconded me as part of their social responsibility in building the country, and in December 1995 I became Director for Personnel Management (HR Director in today's terminology) in the new Department of Labour.

My directorate was responsible for remuneration and benefits, training and development, labour relations, and all HR administration. Anything related to HR for the Department's employees was under my section. One of HR's biggest jobs at the time was rationalising – which meant integrating and in many cases downsizing – all the people and agencies from the former homelands into a single national department.

Employees from the former homelands were coming to Pretoria to join one Department of Labour, and we had to standardise everything from pay scales to conditions of service. For example, people in different homelands had been paid vastly different amounts for the same position, and now those who were paid more were going to have to take pay cuts. Others had been receiving outrageous perks like massive entertainment budgets, luxurious medical aid packages and travel allowances, and those expectations also had to be managed as these things could not be replicated. The pace and amount of work was unprecedented.

Leading from the front

WITH MANDELA AS PRESIDENT, everyone from the Minister down to the lowest level employee gave their absolute best, and in the three short years from 1995 to 1998, the DoL developed no less than six major pieces of legislation. These included the Basic Conditions of Employment Act, the Skills Development Act (which included SETAs), the Employment Equity Act, the Labour Relations Act, the Unemployment Insurance Act (UIF), and the Workman's Compensation Act, as well as establishing the CCMA (Commission for Conciliation, Mediation, and Arbitration). Being in the department, I was privy to seeing how each piece of legislation was so painstakingly developed, then passed in Parliament, and finally implemented. It was definitely one of the most satisfying and intellectually stretching times in my work career. I was working side by side with my friend and colleague Mpho Makwana, who was the Director of Equal Opportunity and who spearheaded the development of the Employment Equity Act of 1998.

This pivotal era in the South African labour market's transformation could not have been headed by a better person than our Director General, Sipho Pityana. I've been very lucky with the leaders I have had, A hard-working and passionate leader, Sipho taught me what it means to lead from the front; in other words, taking bold steps, walking your talk, always putting more effort in than you ask of your employees, and how to get the best from your people by showing them their own capacity for greatness.

Sipho was the kind of leader who generously shared great ideas with his staff, empowering us to make the most of an idea, and always letting us shine in the resulting limelight of success. I recall one incident soon after my arrival at the Department. I was not reporting directly to Sipho but he kept in touch with most of us, regardless of the level we were operating at. At the time, government staff from the homelands were pouring in to Pretoria. Sipho passed by my office one day and said, "There are so many people coming in. Why don't you form a reception committee?" I asked what he meant. "As people come in to Pretoria, everything is new to them. The province is new, the department is new. Why don't you create something that will help ensure that they feel supported by the Department?" He shared more ideas about this concept.

So I established a welcoming committee to receive and integrate staff from the former homelands into the new DoL. That reception committee assisted people with overcoming the difficulties and stresses they faced due to all the changes and uncertainties, both professional (given the restructuring) and personal (given their relocation). In circumstances where people might have otherwise felt scared and isolated, that committee instead made people feel like they belonged to something new and exciting. For example, whenever someone relocated to Pretoria, we allocated time for that person to organise important aspects of their personal lives, like finding schools or childcare facilities, so that they felt free to bring their best to a workplace that supported them. Colleagues in the DoL thought I was so clever, constantly thanking me, but it was the boss's idea. Some even went to the extent of telling him how great I was, but he never did let on that that was his idea.

When I think of Sipho as a leader and multiplier of talent, two major things stand out for me. First, he pushed us hard but was always there to support us. Second, he knew how to acknowledge good work and build people up. Because of his management style, I never felt like I was working hard. Just by who he was, he made me want to give my all. He was a classic example of a multiplier. As Wiseman and McKeown describe in their book, *Multipliers: How the Best Leaders Make Everyone Smarter*, a multiplier is a leader who makes everyone around him or her smarter and better. The following five principles distinguish multipliers – the ability to:

1.   attract talented people and use them at their highest point of contribution;

2.   create an intense workplace that demands people's best thinking and work;

3.   define an opportunity that causes people to stretch;

4.   drive sound decisions through rigorous debate; and

5.   give other people ownership of the results and invest in their success[14].

Sipho did all of these things and more. His extremely high expectations and support elevated my own understanding of what service excellence in government meant. In my view, he was a visionary; he is still breaking barriers even today as one of the founders of the Council for the Advancement of the South African Constitution (CASAC).

Legislating Equity

THE EMPLOYMENT EQUITY ACT was a cornerstone of the transformation legislation developed at this time. Intended to bring equity to South Africa's labour market, the Act was developed in the most deliberate and thoughtful process. One thing that I often find myself explaining about the Act is the value of its strategic use of **targets rather than quotas**. A quota is non-negotiable, focusing on a desired percentage to be achieved, and is often based on 'hard' numbers like demographics, without necessarily considering things like the availability of skills.

---

[14] Wiseman, L. & McKeown, G. 2013. *Multipliers: How the best leaders make everyone smarter.* New York, NY: HarperCollins.

By contrast, as elaborated in the EE Act, targets were to be set by companies for themselves, and with explicit consideration of the pool of available skills. In other words, the Employment Equity Act clearly says that companies must set targets, but they should base those targets on the pool of available resources, and ultimately it is up to a company to determine its own target. For example, let's say you set a target that 10% of your staff will be women. Government knows that the market actually can provide more than 10%, but government will not argue with the number you set. However, you must meet the target you set for yourself.

At its base, the Employment Equity Act was government's way to ensure that every company had a plan in place to integrate greater numbers of previously disadvantaged people into their organisations. Every company needed to create its own EE plan, the plan needed set targets, and the plan needed to be publicised and accessible to all employees. Plenty of companies submitted plans where targets were clearly lower than what the market could provide, but government accepted them. The focus was on getting companies to make a plan and then work on meeting those targets. There were consequences only for companies that failed to develop a plan, lied about their plan (for example, stating that they had 15% female or black employees while their base was far lower), or did not achieve the plan they set for themselves within the specified timeframe.

I personally find the legislation to be fair and balanced. It provides for a reasonable accommodation of transformation strategies, while also taking into account the challenges faced by both companies and the country. Overall, the Act tried to anticipate and accommodate the difficulties companies would face in trying to implement it, which was key because government needed buy-in and adherence, but it also needed an Act with teeth.

In my view, the problems that have been raised about EE come down to poor implementation. For example, one of the biggest complaints has been that the EE Act encourages token appointments, forcing companies to fire white people and replace them with black people. Yet nowhere in the EE Act does it say a company needs to fire white people. In fact, the Act states clearly that it must be implemented in line with the Labour Relations Act, which prevents unilateral dismissal for the sake of EE. However, what we *have* seen is that as a result of poor or lazy implementation – trying to 'get the numbers' without doing the hard work of real transformation – companies struggle with inappropriate hires and then blame it on EE.

This gap between good legislation and the way it is implemented – and the corresponding problem of the legislation itself being blamed – is by no means unique to the EE Act. I will talk more about the problems of the EE Act implementation and how those problems have impacted companies' ability to transform in Chapter 10.

The challenge of inclusion

THERE WERE SO MANY LEVELS at which the challenge of inclusion guided and was present in our work at the DoL. On the broadest level, there was such a keen awareness that all the different pieces of EE legislation being developed would act as the legal basis to validate and support the importance of equity and inclusion in our labour market. Meanwhile, my HR directorate needed to directly address the challenge of inclusion in the process of unifying the multiple agencies and departments that had grown up under the homelands systems, creating one government where systems, expectations, and benefits would be standardised and fair.

Both of these processes – creating the legislation and rationalising the department itself – required that we accommodate everyone, from white staff from the previous government, to black staff from the former homelands, to all the unions, and find a way to carve out a future for our country together.

The legislation in particular needed to reflect both our diversity as a nation, and act as a guide for the way questions of diversity would be treated in this shared future. In all of our efforts at the DoL we **recognised diversity as far more than just race and gender,** trying to always accommodate diversity of thought, perspective, political background, geographical location, and even the systems people had been operating in prior to 1994. From all these differences, we had to come up with a product – meaning a coherent and unified DoL – and a set of laws to guide the rest of the country in terms of transforming the labour market to truly reflect and embrace our nation's diversity.

The EE team made such an effort to ensure that the legislation itself was equitable, focusing on the fact that people had to be treated equitably from the start, hence the name Employment Equity. The process behind the drafting of the legislation required immense sensitivity from leadership, and our Minister and DG took great pains to listen to everyone's views. Arriving at a healthy balance between institutional memory and new blood coming in was so delicate, and it took great wisdom and restraint to recognise and extract value from both.

Striking this balance is exactly what companies that want to transform today must still do, and it is never easy. For example, an organisation should not place too much importance on the people who have years of experience at the expense of new people who can provide an external lens on the organisation, bringing new ideas and perspectives. I think the key to success – then and now – lies more in **creating a space for people to feel they belong** and their opinions are valued and matter, than it is about creating any one specific programme (or piece of legislation). Programmes will follow, but if leadership fails to create a space where mutual respect and appreciation for differences can flourish, they will never get transformation right.

In fact, the challenges faced by government in terms of incorporating and getting the most out of South Africa's diverse perspectives have not really changed much today; the big difference now is whether or not our leadership still has the patience to co-create meaningful and inclusive solutions that speak to our diverse reality.

HAVING COME FROM ESKOM'S ENVIRONMENT where I had a certain view of how race affected rank, I was surprised to find that in government, rank was fundamental in itself. A DG was like a demi-god. People respected level, not colour. As such, despite being a black woman, my seniority as a director ensured that Afrikaans men respected my authority. If I said something they took it seriously, so that was a huge adjustment. Although it was nice to feel so respected regardless of colour, I found that a culture of hierarchy can also limit innovation. For example, if I was in a meeting and I challenged someone, no one would challenge me back because of my position. So that's the downside. The upside was that I never had to question if I was respected because I was a woman or black. In the end, everything in that environment was focused on the work, and everyone – black and white –

was under tremendous pressure to get the legislation out. Our Minister and DG were non-negotiable around deadlines, and there was no time to bicker.

At the same time, realising how my seniority was respected, I used my rank to ensure that the culture of my own directorate was transforming. I sat in on all interviews, even at the entry level. No position went through without me knowing who was on the shortlist, and knowing whether my staff had tried hard enough to find black or female candidates with the right skills. By sitting in on the interviews I ensured that we found good diverse talent – excuses were not entertained. As a result, I was able to promote transformation while recruiting the best talent to my directorate.

Visions and Values

ONE OF THE LESSONS that really came through for me at the DoL was how **a common vision** created and articulated by strong leaders is the foundation of organisational transformation. Our vision at the DoL cascaded down from the President himself (who was Nelson Mandela at the time). It centred on the need for reconciliation on the one hand, and visible change on the other. When everyone is working towards a common goal, extreme workloads and pressurised timelines can be managed with ease. The important thing is to have clarity about where you are heading. Meanwhile, the tangible products that we were developing motivated and encouraged everyone to redouble their efforts when needed.

The massive benefits of a shared vision also hold true for transformation initiatives in any company today. I have worked with many organisations seeking to develop a Transformation Vision, or a statement describing what their organisation's ideal environment should look like. For this vision to transmit and translate at every level, it is necessary that the organisation's leaders have rolled up their sleeves with you in its formulation. The Minister and DG were utterly involved in the DoL's journey, always leading from the front, giving direction, and expecting and receiving the highest levels of delivery from those who worked for them. Being able to follow the roadmap provided by a shared vision was critical here.

Another key part of organisational transformation is the values of the leaders; leadership is not just about the head and what you say – so much of it is about the heart and the things you do and value. **Values are like fingerprints that you leave all over the place in your leadership and life journey.** Instead of spending time convincing people that you are principled, that you hate corruption, or that you lead with integrity – just do it. People will notice.

One of the values that clearly came across from our leadership was the value and necessity of hard work. In my life I've never worked as hard as I did at the DoL. I am well aware of the stereotype of public servants as lazy, but my experience of government was exactly the opposite, and I suspect it had everything to do with our leadership, from the President (Nelson Mandela) to the Deputy President (Thabo Mbeki), Minister (Tito Mboweni) and Director General. Given how much the DoL was responsible for at that time – the creation of all the new legislation, the rationalisation process, the establishment of the CCMA and the SETAs[15] – it is clear that a strong work ethic is not about where you work (i.e. government or private sector) but about the values and high-performance culture, which are shaped by the leadership.

Our leaders were the ones who created a culture in which excellence was non-negotiable. Having colleagues of the calibre of Mpho and Sipho with whom to bounce ideas around and share strategies was incredibly rewarding, and the environment that their leadership created was the perfect space for advancing transformation in our country. Additionally, during my time at the DoL many very senior ANC leaders were still alive and we had a lot of wisdom to draw from. Working in government back then was like being in the engine room where a dream was being built. The job demanded that I grow by leaps and bounds, and I found it extremely personally gratifying. I was 30 years old and every day I looked forward to going to work and giving my all.

---

[15] SETA stands for 'Sector Education and Training Authority'. SETAs include employers, trade unions, government departments, and bargaining councils from each industrial sector. The Skills Development Act (1998) provided the framework for the development of skills in the workplace.

INSIGHTS & TIPS

Just as my early work experiences confirmed the value of mentorship, my time at the Department of Labour firmly established the importance of leaders who walk the talk and lead from the front. This type of leadership is critical for the success of transformation and diversity initiatives. I also witnessed and participated first-hand in shaping our nation's first employment equity legislation. While often misapplied and misunderstood, this legislation was painstakingly developed and is still the cornerstone for building an equitable labour market.

The importance of leading from the front

Be visible and support transformation efforts with your 'Head', 'Heart' and 'Hands'

 Practical Tips

- Leadership must show that they are non-negotiable in their expectations of excellence, and must demonstrate values and ethics in their approach to transformation.

- As a leader, be very conscious of how you talk about Employment Equity and related legislation. Critically reflect on how your organisation has correctly or incorrectly implemented the Act, rather than criticising the legislation.

- As a leadership team, spend time carefully developing a Transformation Vision for your organisation. Visualise what you would like your organisation to look like in the future.

- Communicate the spirit of the Act and your organisation's transformation vision, strategy and plan to dispel myths, negative attitudes and fears that EE is intended to disadvantage one group in order to benefit another. This is simply not true.

- Be hands-on in creating the culture of your organisation. Leaders set the standard through their own personal transformation, showing what is and is not allowed.

- Be aware that a leader's values will permeate the organisation and the products it creates or the services it delivers.

Building and multiplying talent

Find the best people and support their growth and development

 Practical Tips

- As leaders, be actively involved in ensuring that your recruitment team is putting in the effort required to recruit the best black and female candidates. Don't settle for easy excuses that they couldn't find diverse candidates.

- Attract talented people and use them at their highest point of contribution.

- Create an intense workplace that demands people's best thinking and work.

- Define opportunities that cause people to stretch and provide them with the support they need to grow and flourish.

- Actively support and promote continuous professional development.

- Drive sound HR decisions through rigorous debate.

- Give other people ownership of the results and invest in their success[16].

---

[16] Wiseman, L. & McKeown, G. 2013. *Multipliers: How the best leaders make everyone smarter.* New York, NY: HarperCollins.

The importance of vision, values and commitment

Model the importance of hard work, commitment and dedicated leadership

 Practical Tips

- Leaders should always strive for a shared vision and a plan to follow to deliver on the vision. This vision needs to be shared with employees at all levels.

- As part of the organisation's vision and values, ensure equity and inclusion at all levels through:

  ◦ the art of listening;

  ◦ balancing institutional memory and new blood; and

  ◦ defining diversity in its broadest terms.

- Create a space of belonging: every person on a team needs to feel they belong on the team and that his or her opinion matters.

- Leaders need to be seen as part of the process (roll up your sleeves and engage with your teams on the transformation journey).

Chapter 7

STUMBLING BLOCKS

Informal Networks and Invisible Power (1997-98)

> A community is divided when their perception
> of the same thing is different.
>
> *Steve Biko*

IN 1997, MARE NORVAL & ASSOCIATES Employment Agency approached me with the possibility of a major promotion to Executive Director of Transformation for the Cape Town City Council. Like the rest of the country, the City of Cape Town was undergoing a huge restructuring. At that stage they were in the midst of amalgamating a number of municipalities – including the iKapa Town Council, which had until then exclusively served black people in the townships – into a unified "One City of Cape Town".

I accepted and was hired as the City's first black female Executive Director. I would be heading a new portfolio called Transformation, with the main focus being to create an effective and smoothly functioning municipality where all residents felt they belonged. I saw the job as a great opportunity to meld my experiences from the rationalising work at the DoL with my growing passion for diversity and transformation work. Upon arrival, however, I faced what turned out to be the highly emotional and complex task of leading transformation in the context of rationalisation.

The idea during the restructuring was that no individual could claim any job, and everyone had to reapply for his or her post. Some left voluntarily, but many stayed to compete for limited posts. For example, each municipality had had its own Director of Housing; now they were all applying for the City's one new Director of Housing position. You can imagine the anxiety.

In my mind, the one thing that mitigated the pain and stress of this process was the opportunity it presented for transformation, but if we wanted to use the restructuring opportunity to progress with the City's transformation goals, we needed to act quickly. Although I expressed this urgency to appoint black people where we could, others were saying that the black candidates from municipalities like iKapa lacked experience. However, my view was that if we didn't appoint people during the process, then five years later when the next opportunity came along, those candidates would still lack experience because we hadn't used this chance to give them the experience they needed. This is often the paradox in transformation work; you can't get a job because of a lack of experience, but how are you supposed to get experience if no one will hire you? It is always easy for people to agree that employment equity is important when there are no vacancies and when they don't have to back up their words with action.

In the end, township candidates played second fiddle, and the City's unofficial default position was to give the jobs to whoever was in the post from the Central Business District (CBD), which generally meant the majority of them would be white males. And so although I thought I was there to help the City capitalise on the rationalisation process and along the way ensure that black and female managers were given consideration, mine turned out to be among a few lone voices.

In the Same Boat?

WHILE IN CAPE TOWN, my interaction showed me how our perception of the word transformation can mean a totally different thing even when we say we are fighting for the same cause. While purporting to drive the transformation agenda, I found many of my colleagues to be exhibiting various forms of unconscious bias that made me wonder how much they really understood.

Jumping forward to our current context, I have observed that in the last five years, the topic of **white privilege** has featured more prominently in South Africa's race debates. I find it greatly encouraging to see white people organising themselves into learning groups and addressing the topic of whiteness and white privilege. These individuals are doing the inner work that I believe is so vital to transformation – that is, educating themselves about how rank, power, and privilege play out in so many aspects of their lives.

From when I was back in Fort Hare, whenever we referred to Cape Town the term 'liberal' came with it, hence my friends said about my departure to UCT that I was going to a 'white liberal institution'. While working for the City of Cape Town in the late 1990s, I encountered a number of people who would have benefitted from frank discussions about white privilege.

Having contributed to the emancipation of the poor through various struggle activities in South Africa, a lot of people saw themselves as advancing the transformation agenda but without doing the 'inner work' of introspection. One of my white female colleagues put it eloquently when she said, "I was so caught up in the 'good white' syndrome that I saw other people being candidates for this type of work- not myself until I had to do serious introspection that I too, despite having always fought for equal rights, have to work through my baggage and unconscious bias as a white South African".

This uncritiqued liberal mind-set can harm transformation work to the extent that it can feed an assumption that people share a collective vision for change and transformation when in fact they do not. The **absence of a clearly articulated and shared vision** made it so clear to me how vital a shared vision is when working on complex social change. When you assume the existence of a shared vision but do not actually develop one, ideas stay in people's heads. As such, you will never really have clarity about what transformation means, and how you can therefore effectively work towards it. Even if you think you all want the same thing, it is very important to put ideas into words so that all your actions can be measured against that vision. Otherwise, the vision is an amoeba whose shape can change depending on who is talking about it.

AUGMENTING THE PROBLEMS resulting from the lack of a clear guiding vision, the complexity of dealing with local government in one of South Africa's biggest cities was a shock to me. I battled to catch up and figure out how things worked. When working at the national level I had primarily interacted with the Minister or DG and the decision-making processes were relatively straightforward. By contrast, in local government there was a whole council at the core of every decision. I was more at the coalface, which was incredibly different and a huge challenge.

Another challenge I faced was the difference represented by my actual person. Being the only and first female Executive Director, being African, being from Johannesburg – all of my diversity markers became so pronounced in the Cape Town environment. This difference fed into a growing assumption from some of my colleagues that I regarded transformation purely as getting black faces in. Although of course race was an integral part of transformation for me, it was certainly not the only thing.

I believed that as we were communicating a 'One City of Cape Town' vision, that oneness should also be reflected in the way the restructuring itself was done. I wanted the end result of the restructuring and amalgamation to reflect evidence of a deliberate effort to take the different municipalities – and all of their racial, gender, and geographic diversity – into account. When I expressed my concerns that we were losing opportunities to transform, I would hear things like, "The business of business is much more than just colour". When you hear such statements you know you're in a complex web that is difficult to untangle. I see the same phenomenon even now with some executives, who try to push the transformation agenda in many organisations and end up being pigeonholed as tunnel-minded and irrelevant. To some extent, I do understand the motivation (although I don't excuse it) of those black or female executives who try to stay far away from the topic of transformation. However, if your job title is Transformation, I offer no easy tips as to where you can hide or avoid the subject.

The power of informal networks and culture

THE FIRST TIME I WALKED INTO the huge hushed offices that grace the top floor of Cape Town's Civic Centre, I immediately noticed the serious shortage of black PAs (personal assistants) on that floor. Given my position as Head of Transformation, I felt I should lead the way, and made a conscious decision to appoint a black PA. I found a suitable candidate with all the skills I needed. We clicked and I hired her. Although she was from Cape Town, she had not previously worked at those levels in the municipality. As it turned out, this last point was a terrible oversight. The way my PA struggled to understand and navigate the system and the culture really demonstrated **the power of informal networks**.

Informal networks are all the personal connections and relationships that exist between people; they are the "grease" that oils the wheels of so many business transactions and interactions. The stronger those connections, the easier it is to execute what you need. When I needed a meeting set up with other senior people, my PA struggled. Or people would confirm, but then closer to the time they would decline. This happened again and again. Meanwhile, the other PAs all knew each other and were even on a first-name basis with the other bosses. They could just say as friends, "Hey, be sure to get your boss to this meeting", and it would happen. My PA's difficulty in organising meetings ultimately affected perceptions of my competence and my work.

Prior to this job I had always thought that when black managers chose white PAs they were not committed to transformation. I had failed to see the reality that sometimes what you need most of all is an 'insider'. The hard truth was that I would have had better success had I hired a white PA in that setting. Not because a white PA would have been more competent (a myth reinforced by situations like mine), but because the informal networks I needed to access were mainly white.

Coming into a big machine like a municipality, those two invisible levels can topple you. I lacked both. I would never have the informal networks because I was from Johannesburg, parachuted into a senior position, had never worked for a municipality, and hired a PA who was also an outsider who had no access to those powerful informal networks. For both my PA and myself, this challenge had nothing to do with not being qualified for the job; I had all the technical qualifications but I lacked a critical aspect called 'the network of relationships', which is never a focus in any recruitment panel discussion. Meanwhile, that very lack exacerbated my unfamiliarity with the culture of the municipality. In any organisation, **culture is not written down on paper**. It is highly possible that you could go through this and a colleague sitting right next to you would be totally oblivious to your struggles. I was often hesitant to explain this to my colleagues for fear of being labelled as petty or nit-picking, yet the impact on my work was enormous. The inner critic and dialogue in my head was, "How do I even begin this conversation? Do I have a problem when people use their long-standing networks and friendships? Do I want to be friends with their friends or what?" Culture is simply the way things are done in a place. When you're new, you'll quickly discover if you have allies to help you, show you the shortcuts, and circumvent certain things. Without those allies – they can be mentors or friendly peers – you will just keep coming up against the otherwise invisible barrier of culture. The invisible and informal system can exclude, despite the formal recruitment objectives of inclusion.

LOOKING BACK, I ASK MYSELF if I could have done something differently to address my lack of access to the informal networks and to better understand the dominant culture operating in the City of Cape Town. I think the first step would have been **talking about it and creating awareness**. Although it would have been uncomfortable, had I made people understand that I was facing this barrier that other (white male) managers did not even have to think about, it might have helped. This brings to the fore the ongoing double-bind dilemma of feeling damned if you do and damned if you don't, which many black people constantly grapple with: must we constantly raise issues of race and unconscious bias? If we do raise the issues, are we feeding the 'all they think about is race' narrative? And if we remain silent, are we colluding with the problem and even potentially allowing the issue to fester? This creates the feeling of a no win situation and that whatever decision you make, you are wrong.

This explains why I frequently talk about the importance of people in a particular context using their rank to help others. People always talk about meritocracy, but when you are part of the 'in group', it can be hard to see that the next person doesn't have the same things you have – not because they are incompetent or lazy, but because they can't access the networks or don't enjoy **the privileges of rank** that you take for granted.

So much unearned privilege goes unrecognised. For example, if your social circles place you at a relaxed Sunday morning brunch at the boss's house, where you and you partner are friendly with the boss and his wife, your kids go to the same school, you participate in the same sporting activities, some even belong to the same lift club etc., you should recognise this as unearned privilege; a person who lacks this access will never enjoy the same ability to discuss important work issues in such a favourable setting. It's not even about playing golf together, which is an example quoted often. There are many scenarios that apply. If my boss and I meet often in social settings, I can go through my important agenda items very informally but effectively. In contrast, my colleague has to phone their PA, set up an appointment and meet the boss in a less favourable formal office or boardroom environment. These are the uncomfortable truths that people don't want to admit, but which must be recognised if meaningful transformation is to come about.

Another thing that could have helped me deal with the challenges of transitioning into an unfamiliar organisation would have been a **broader support system**. As we had in the DoL for staff coming from the former homelands, if there had been some kind of support system to assist me as an employee coming from a different province, it would have helped immensely. Challenges faced by people who are new to the system can be multi-layered. There are the professional structural challenges (e.g. figuring out how local government structures function), as well as the personal social challenges (e.g. relocating to a new city). How ironic that in the DoL the reception committee that I was leading assisted many, but in the City of Cape Town, I was the one in need of such a service.

Those who are willing to help can reach out to newer employees and give them access to their informal networks. This kind of system would also apply to multinationals that want to give opportunities to employees to work in different countries; having established a structured programme to help them adjust to a foreign setting is important to their success and productivity. These are practical things that leadership can and should recognise and address.

Without the power of informal networks and culture to support you, your position can become an empty box; your qualifications and competencies cease to matter. The truth is that even within meritocracies, we all need someone to hold our hand and show us the ropes in order to succeed. I don't care who you are, when you enter a new system, success hinges on someone walking the journey with you and having your back.

Stranger in a strange land

THE ISOLATION I FELT AT WORK was mirrored in my personal life in Cape Town. I couldn't help but feel that as someone from Gauteng, I was always going to be seen as a visitor or outsider.

People often want you to 'prove' such feelings when you mention them, but how do I prove a feeling? I can tell you how when I walked through town, I didn't see the kaleidoscope of South African cultures that I was used to in Johannesburg. Or I could tell you about the time some black friends from Johannesburg were visiting and we went to a posh restaurant, and the (black) security guy at the door said, "Surely you are not from here. You must be from Johannesburg or Durban". When I asked why he would say that, he told me, "Black people don't come here". That was so surprising to me at the time. Or I could tell you how vividly I remember the lack of other black people in my neighbourhood, the beautiful and central suburb of Tamboerskloof. In fact, this absence should not have surprised me given how I acquired that apartment.

When I first arrived in Cape Town I phoned around but struggled to find an available apartment. Finally, my white friend, Mare Norval, who originally recruited me into the Cape Town job, phoned the same agency I had been calling, and the very same day she secured the place I wanted. Mare, whom I regard as a real activist and always willing to challenge such unfairness, was really not impressed with the agency. It is amazing how she continues to play this role, not only for me but for many who need such intervention. Even as I write this, I cannot help but feel like sometimes it is not good to feel like someone is 'fighting for you'; while it is appreciated and needed, it's not a great feeling. Although I liked my flat, there was a bitterness in knowing that I lived there because of a favour. Such things automatically tell you that you are not welcome. On being asked in a *City View* interview what he saw as Cape Town's greatest challenge in 2012, Prof Njabulo Ndebele said, "I think that the next big challenge for Cape Town is what I would call paying attention to the human fabric in the quilt that the Western Cape is putting together. I would like to see more people who come into the city being able to see something of themselves in it – from those living in the CBD, to those living further afield in our city and our country, and those coming from the African continent and the world. Achieving this is a tremendous challenge, but also a gift that the city can give".

LOUISE HAY TALKS ABOUT how **your body gives you warning signals**. I remember during that period having coffee with a friend visiting from Johannesburg. He asked if I was happy. When I said no, he told me he could see it. My body was beginning to show signs – I was getting ill all the time. At one point, I was so depressed I even looked for a psychologist. I had never experienced this kind of unhappiness in a job.

When I talk about how diversity and inclusion is so much more than just 'getting black faces', one of the things I am referring to is the need for leadership and management to **actively listen and look for the not-so-obvious**. If you tune in and pay attention to the people around you, you can pick up when people are not well. Physical signs like constant neck pain, stiff muscles, and knots in the stomach that are not easy to explain can actually be manifestations of depression and anxiety. Even now when I see these signs in people, it reminds me of myself at that time.

I was not making it in Cape Town. Despite my otherwise excellent track record, I was beginning to question my own competence. When you reach this point in a job, I believe it is better to take care of yourself; if you stay in the environment that is making you feel this way, you will only gather more evidence confirming how little you know. When people talk about **how exclusion and isolation can impact performance**, I have such deep empathy due to this negative experience.

I had stayed in Cape Town exactly one year when I resigned. Just one year was all it took to make me feel I had been an imposter all along. Looking back, I think of Maya Angelou's comment about how even after writing so many books, she still suffered from 'imposter syndrome'. Women, especially female leaders, so often suffer from this syndrome, which is that inner critic saying you're not as good as you think. For me, imposter syndrome meant that I started to think I really didn't know anything about transformation. Even under normal circumstances that voice is often there, but now due to the negative feedback I had been getting from the whole system around me, I started to believe it.

THE ONE GIFT I CAN OFFER people who are going through an experience like this is to say you can get out. The best way to start to heal is by **admitting how hurt and affected you are** to someone who will listen. There were instances where I had really come to believe this story about myself. I thought, "In fact they are right, I know nothing, I am an imposter". That insecurity is like a cancer – once the notion takes hold, it can grow and grow until you isolate and excise it.

There are a lot of perceptions around why people leave organisations. The dominant narrative is that it is for money or a better opportunity. While those may both be true, the underlying reasons often have to do with the culture, lack of support, and fatigue in dealing with a dominant culture that is unwilling to change. For this reason, I believe it is important to look for innovative ways to retain staff. As opposed to the traditional exit interviews, conducting staying interviews may help unravel the problems before they reach breaking point. The facilitation of those dialogue sessions require skill, as observing the passion and intensity of someone's answer might give you pointers to follow up.

AS YOU CAN IMAGINE, I felt the most tremendous relief after I handed in my resignation letter. I received a call informing me that I had been awarded a British Council Scholarship to study for my MBA in the UK. It felt like God had answered my prayers – I was so happy.

INSIGHTS & TIPS

On reflection, I personally don't think my role in the City of Cape Town was very effective – there were too many dynamics to deal with; too many hurdles to overcome. The need for a solid support system was so real – both in the workplace and at home. The pain I experienced during that time gave me a lasting sense of empathy for others fighting similar battles, a great awareness of the power of informal networks, and a desire to help organisations develop a shared vision for true inclusion.

The importance of an articulated and shared vision

Don't make assumptions about having a collective vision

 Practical Tips

- As a leadership team, engage in facilitated conversations around your definitions of transformation, diversity and inclusion. Be open to other views and be willing to share your own.

- Define your organisation's transformation vision, and make sure there is collective buy-in through allowing employees at all levels to give input into the vision.

- When you are debating what your vision should be and how to achieve it, use hard facts rather than basing arguments on emotions and subjective opinions. For example, if I show that the profile of managers at a particular level is 80% white male and my job is to drive employment equity, it is reasonable for me to insist that we open more positions for black people.

The power of the invisible: informal networks and culture

Use your rank positively to support employees and create access for all

 Practical Tips

- If you have rank, be willing to share your networks with new colleagues. Introduce them to the leaders and influential people in your organisation and amongst your stakeholders.

- Recognise unearned privilege and be careful of making quick judgements about another person's merit or lack thereof.

- Understand your organisation's culture and how set and established it may be. If you are in the middle of a rationalisation or transformation process, be very aware that the dominant culture can still take over. Push for diversity to be a priority as part of the change process.

- Create support groups for new staff, especially people relocating to a new province or area. This can include buddy systems where new employees are paired with a buddy or mentor who already has experience within the organisation.

- Assess the extent to which there is a broader support system for the growth and well-being of all your employees, at all levels.

- Talk about the hard or uncomfortable things. People need to be allowed to express their fears. But also, especially during change processes, people need to understand that managers have to make hard decisions (such as firing people, rationalisation processes, etc.).

- Be alert to and mitigate the disconnect that can exist between the formal aspects of an organisation's systems (e.g. policies and procedures that aim to include, such as roles, structures, recruitment, employment equity etc.) and the informal system (e.g. the network of relationships, conversations and the sources of informal power and influence).

The challenges associated with Employment Equity

Recognise that EE is hard to enact but be willing to take bold steps

 ## Practical Tips

- Recognise the fact that people only gain experience through being an appointment to a position, and in order to get that experience one must be appointed first.

- Accept that all appointments come with risks. In EE appointments there are also bound to be mistakes, but do not let those mistakes define what you do.

- Be conscious of the tendency to always associate the word 'black' with 'potential'. There are so many black people who are qualified and can step into a position now, not just 'potentially'.

- Be careful of generalisations and choice of words when speaking about race groups, transformation or other diversity issues. For example, comments like the following can be very damaging: "Look at what *they* have done, *they've* messed up government."

The pain of exclusion

Pro-actively confront your own experiences of exclusion and those of others

 ## Practical Tips

- Don't underestimate the pain of exclusion or of being undermined, but also remember that you can recover by identifying someone you can trust and talk to about your experience. Sometimes a coach or a counsellor can be of great help.

- Conduct stay interviews: understand why people might want to leave your organisation before they hand over their resignation letter if you really want to create an inclusive culture.

- Be aware that sometimes the reasons an individual leaves your organisation may be affecting more people than just the one who has left. Analysing these responses is a responsible way of leading for inclusion.

- It can be helpful to conduct a second exit interview three months after an employee has left your organisation.

- If you are experiencing or have experienced 'imposter syndrome', where the environment has led you to question your own abilities and competencies, admit to someone how hurt you are and realise that it can take a long time to recover. Be patient with the process of healing.

Chapter 8

ON MY OWN

Mandate Molefi (1998-2005)

> The poorest person in the world is not the one without
> money but the one without vision.
>
> *Ghanaian Proverb*

I RETURNED TO JOHANNESBURG to a house I had purchased in my Eskom days. With the prospect of my departure overseas, I accepted a short-term consulting contract to tide me over until my studies began. The firm was called Mandate HR, and its owners, Heather Price and Arlene Ketz, were people I had hired to run diversity workshops back at Eskom. Mandate HR's training content was very much aligned with what I had been learning in the USA at the time, and I liked the professionalism with which Heather and Arlene ran their company. When Heather heard I was back in Johannesburg she asked if I was interested in consulting for them.

It was 1998 and the Employment Equity Act had just come into effect. It was important that companies be guided on how to start the process of transformation, since many did not know what that really meant. Mandate HR had just landed a big contract with a mining company to develop and implement a transformation strategy. Although we had been selected on the basis of our knowledge of diversity, the fact that we modelled the very diversity under discussion was obviously a big bonus, and Heather was very keen for me to be involved at every stage.

As a result, my first big job as a consultant at Mandate HR was to co-present the initial transformation strategy – a key presentation explaining what was a very new and important topic in South Africa at the time. Heather had trained me on her approach and I understood it well, but when we got to the client and I stood up before the senior team, I suddenly found myself perspiring and struggling to breathe. The room went still as I stood there shaking and biting my tongue. I was having an anxiety attack.

I could feel tension and mild embarrassment emanating from some of the black people in the audience. "You are a monumental flop", was what my head was telling me. Heather saw what was happening and took over, which was both a relief and a problem. I say it was a problem because it triggered a voice in my head saying, "You had to be rescued". But if you asked me for a better solution today, I wouldn't be able to tell you what it should have been.

The residue of hurt, self-doubt and the onset of internalised oppression

When I talk about the long-term effects of exclusion and **how feelings of inadequacy can undermine your abilities**, this is exactly what I mean. Where was the confidence I had always enjoyed? I had to own up to and deal with the psychological fall-out from my job in Cape Town. Heather was amazingly supportive, but when you have certain narratives in your head – in this case, 'I am not good enough, I am an imposter!' and 'Do I really know this subject?' – it doesn't matter how much you know or how competent you are. Insecurity can really bring you down.

With time, I regained my confidence. Doing so required me to keep presenting, leading workshops and trainings, and getting myself back out there. About two months after that anxiety attack, I went to present the results of a culture survey at a financial institution. I was presenting directly to the CEO and his team, and I was on top of my game. I owned that presentation and it felt so good. From that day on I knew the baggage of insecurity that I had taken on in Cape Town was mostly gone. Even so, if I am being completely honest, I must admit to a residue that lingered much later, but I learned to control it; to acknowledge the voice of the inner critic and then turn its volume down and turn up the volume of the 'new me' – which was actually the real me who just got derailed along the way. My consulting work provided new positive data and emotionally corrective experiences for me to draw on to counteract that negativity. If I felt nervous I could remind myself about a presentation I had done brilliantly just the previous week, and tell myself that there was nothing stopping me from carrying on. By **identifying my problem and naming it** – that is, how demoralised I had become in my job in Cape Town – I could minimise its power over me.

During those initial months of consulting for Mandate HR, I received the disappointing news that my scholarship would not cover the costs of bringing my 4-year-old daughter with me overseas. Deciding to turn that opportunity down was one of the most difficult choices I have had to make, but I knew what it was like to not have a mother, and even if it was only for one year, I could not leave my child behind. Fortunately I was enjoying the consulting work and I decided to stay on.

In Business

I HAD BEEN AT MANDATE HR for two years when I became a partner in the business. Arlene had been focusing more on HR training and less on diversity work, and she was planning to leave to start a new company. I never intended to be an entrepreneur but the opportunity presented itself, and thus Mandate Molefi was born. I lacked the capital but we agreed I could pay for my share of the company through business that I brought in; it took three years to pay the whole thing off. During that time I remember a lot of my colleagues and friends were saying that Heather should just give me the 50% without paying because I brought my 'blackness' to the company, but that never sat well with me.

By 2003 I had paid in full for my shares. The onset of the new democratic dispensation had demanded a broadening and deepening of our services to stay relevant, and our focus at Mandate Molefi was very clearly on Employment Equity strategies, diversity, and culture change.

Even though the Employment Equity Act had been promulgated in 1998, companies still did not really understand what it meant or how to comply with it. Many companies were 'talking' transformation, but evidence of real effort beyond intentions of 'getting black faces' was mostly lacking. Many companies adopted a 'transformation is good for business' narrative, but it soon became clear that most did not know what they meant by that statement. Helping organisations to define this for themselves became a new guiding approach to our work.

Meanwhile, not long after I had paid off my 50% share of the business, Heather started talking about immigrating and now wanted to sell her share of the business. Suddenly I had to raise the funds to become the sole proprietor of a growing enterprise. This time, however, I needed to come up with the cash to buy her out all at once.

Despite the fact that I was buying my partner out of an already existing business, accessing funds proved an enormous challenge. I went to all the banks but not one would give me a loan. The trouble I faced was partly due to the fact that Mandate Molefi was a service business, and so the banks questioned what exactly it was that they were funding. But it was more than that. The banks told me that the success of the business was 'brand dependent', and with one partner leaving, they worried about my ability to attract enough business on my own (what do you think I was reading in between the lines?). The unspoken subtext was that the departing partner was the white partner, and how would a black owner manage alone? The irony of this – given that ours was the business of transformation – was not lost on me. I so vividly remember the pain of looking for a loan and repeatedly coming up empty.

Getting a loan can be a challenge for any new business, but even now I see how much more difficult it is for women to get the backing of established financial institutions. Of course for black women it is that much harder still. I am often confronted by this reality when doing public speaking engagements on women in leadership or transformation. Participants constantly tell me that it is well and good that government talks about all these great initiatives to give women priority in terms of empowerment loans and contracts, but their own experience is a far cry from the 'fairy tale' being spun. My own experience concurs.

In the end, I finally got a personal loan from a connection, from an owner in the shipping industry. To pay that loan back I had to come up with a significant amount every month for three years straight. It was incredibly difficult at times, but I never defaulted. To this day, I am proud that I serviced that loan well.

My tough journey with the banks gave me first-hand experience of what most would-be entrepreneurs go through. My experience also highlighted the **degree to which business success can be about access to networks,** and makes me wonder how many give up on their dreams because of a lack of access to funds. Despite my own challenges, when all was said and done, I found myself the proud sole owner of a growing business.

Sole Proprietor

AS IT TURNED OUT, getting my loan was just the first of many challenges I faced as a black female business owner. When some of our existing clients heard that Heather had left, they followed suit. Here I had just taken on this massive debt, and a top client cancelled the project we had agreed on just a few weeks prior. I was terrified.

The biggest moment of discrimination that I experienced after Heather left was still to come though. Before Heather's departure the bank manager we worked with would hold our debit orders whenever needed, but after Heather left, my bank drastically dropped my overdraft. For an ongoing period they continuously wanted to review and downgrade me. And of course the more I was in trouble, the worse my profile became. I was constantly on edge during that lonely time, which really highlighted how tough it was to be a black entrepreneur. That was when, as a businessperson, I had to ask, "Am I bold or stupid?" I decided to be bold. In addition to the day-to-day running of things and delivering on contracts, I worked tirelessly to market and promote the business.

For those people lucky enough to have never experienced such **difficulties of entry into business** or sustaining yourself in business, it is so important to understand that this is what other people face on a regular basis. And for those of you out there who are going through similar experiences, I bring this up to highlight how many before you have gone through the same thing, and to encourage you to hold on. This was a time when I had to have a strong anchor; something larger than me to look up to and gain strength from. In my case, my belief in God centred me.

In addition, what helped me hold on was my passion for my work and my deep sense of meaning and pride to be contributing to the overall transformation of our country. Knowing that I was facilitating dialogue to heal the wounds of the past and helping organisations seek solutions to carve a new path forward kept me going. In addition, the unsolicited feedback and thank you notes that I received from participants across racial and gender lines – people whom I had trained, helped to better understand themselves, and for whom I had provided tools for coping with this complex change – were also incredibly motivating.

AT THE SAME TIME that I was dealing with my company's financial concerns, there were perceptions that I had gotten the business for free and was benefitting from affirmative action or the BEE (Black Economic

Empowerment) legislation that was instituted in 2003. The people who said such things had no idea how I had paid for my shares, or how I lost clients when my white partner left. People assumed I got business easily, but the reality was that I struggled doubly hard. As a successful black businessperson, you often have to **deal with the perception that you get contracts because of Broad-Based Black Economic Empowerment (B-BBEE) ratings**, as opposed to being given them because of your competence.

Despite the irritation I sometimes felt when these assumptions were turned towards me, I still believe in the importance of the legislation, which expanded in 2007 with B-BBEE. There is a lot of misinformation about what B-BBEE is. In essence, B-BBEE, which was first initiated in 2003 as BEE, was intended to help transform the economy to better represent the demographics of the country. It was expanded in 2007 to the current point system, which incentivises companies to hire and use businesses owned or managed by 'previously disadvantaged' groups, including black people, coloured people, Indian people, women, etc.

Very simply, the way it works is that every company with an annual turnover greater than R10 million should have a B-BBEE rating, which is based on how much your organisation empowers previously disadvantaged people in business. Points are based on things like the percentage of black owners/managers/shareholders; how much business you give to black- and women-owned or managed companies; the level of professional development you offer employees, etc.

In order to work with public entities or qualify for large contracts like government tenders, you need to have a good B-BBEE rating. For big companies like financial services and medical aid businesses, having a good B-BBEE rating is vital if you want to operate at a certain level. Even for smaller companies that do not rely on government tenders, having a good B-BBEE rating is a point of credibility and eligibility for certain tax benefits and financial grants. Although B-BBEE compliance is voluntary, having a poor rating – which results from things like not developing your staff or not procuring any services from black-owned companies – essentially makes it hard to compete in South Africa's formal business sector. Although B-BBEE has certainly been helpful and I agree with it in principle, its existence far from guarantees one's success as a black businesswoman.

B-BBEE or not, those early months were hard for me, and there were times when my company's balance sheet was in the red. I hadn't fully appreciated how long it can take just to talk about a proposal with a client, never mind actually getting to the point where they sign you on. On top of the usual difficulties of signing clients that I had experienced when working with Heather, I saw how **as a black woman, entry was that much more difficult**. The amount of time, energy, and effort I needed to convince potential clients that I could do a job had certainly more than doubled. If there had ever been a time to give up, it was then.

Slowly but surely, however, I did get new clients. This experience taught me that **it is okay to be scared: sometimes you have to feel the fear and just carry on anyway**. My persistence paid off. Within three years, my turnover had quadrupled. In the end, success – in life or in business – is about resilience. That said, even after I signed a deal, I still had to negotiate the biases and frustrating behaviours of black and white clients alike.

Black, female and in charge

WHEN DEALING WITH CLIENTS, I regularly face various struggles particular to being black, being a woman, or both. One of the first things I started to notice was that **I was (and still am) always asked for a discount**. As soon as I quote my fee, I receive this sense of, 'How can you cost so much?' Don't get me wrong: I've given and requested many discounts – that is part of business – but I can tell the difference between someone who negotiates with everyone versus someone who thinks a black company should be cheaper. And I should mention that I get this reaction equally or sometimes even more from potential black clients. You see it in the way people ask. Once when I gave my rate to a potential client she said, "Even an advocate doesn't charge that". So I asked what she was comparing, because the service I offer is an entirely different field than what she was comparing it to.

I get concerned when I get the sense that by virtue of being black I'm perceived as 'too expensive'. I have white colleagues who are friends and I know what they charge. So I know the issue is not that I am too expensive, but rather that there is this expectation that a black company should be cheaper, or that I should be grateful that I am even getting an opportunity to work.

The comment I hear most frequently after I've been asked for a discount is, "Be smart – if you drop your price, you will get your foot in, then once you are in you can demand what you think you are worth". I can tell you categorically that this will never happen. Once you lock yourself into a particular costing model (especially when it is below market value), even if you do an excellent job, you cannot suddenly increase your price by 200%. It would never make sense to any procurement manager. A policy book would be thrown at you, and in most cases, the very person who convinced you to drop your prices will refer you to the procurement department for any further discussions on financial matters. I learned this lesson the hard way, and treasure the hard-won knowledge.

Yet I should also claim my part in this – having internalised how clients responded to black consultants, at some point I realised I was offering a discount before I was even asked for it. That's when I did my own inner work and asked what I was doing. My brain had learned what was expected of a black consultant ('you need to be thankful, you need to be grateful for the work'), and so even if my conscious mind disagreed, I had adopted this tendency. So there was a time when I bought the story as well.

Another related problem I have encountered is the reluctance of some clients to give a big contract to a black consultant. **Many organisations are more comfortable giving black companies piecemeal contracts**. The accompanying comments are similar to the rationale for undercutting your price: "This small piece of work will open other doors for you" or "We will give you more work later". Again, this theme hinges on the notion that I should be grateful to be working at all. Moving past the issue of the unconscious bias underlying that thinking, this kind of piecemeal contracting can limit and negatively impact the model you can implement, and so again serves to perpetuate misconceptions about the capabilities of black consultants.

Pushback and Internalised Oppression

ONE OF THE BIGGEST ISSUES I face as a black female consultant presenting to potential clients concerns the need to **answer fear-based pushback on transformation**. I most often experience this in the initial stages of meeting with clients, and the experience varies depending on the level of self-awareness of the people involved – what I call the 'broker client' versus the 'power client' – and the nature of their relationship to one another.

In my line of work, a broker client is someone from a company's HR department – a Transformation Manager or Learning and Development (LD) Manager – while the power client is a company's CEO or Managing Director (MD). Although I have worked with powerful broker clients who are firm, fair and 'speak truth to power', I have also encountered broker clients who are not very highly regarded by the power clients. If as a transformation consultant you are first introduced to a company through a broker client who is not highly regarded, you already have a disadvantage. In this scenario, various things tend to happen: the broker client passes their insecurity on to you, and/or wants you to promise heaven and earth to make up for their own fears and lack of regard by the CEO, MD or other members of the executive committee.

Over the years of fighting discrimination, I have found this kind of **scenario** all too common, and it comes across as internalised oppression on the part of the broker client. Internalised oppression is when you believe the negative stereotypes about your group, and then act in ways that are limiting to yourself or others of your group. You can feel it when someone is asking you questions laced with internalised oppression or insecurity. For example, "Tell me, how are you going to convince white males that there is value in this thing?" Or, "Tell me, how are you going to get all of Exco to believe in you?"

If you sense that you are merely answering a broker client's fears, often based on his or her internalised oppression, know that your path is already tainted; you will be walking on eggshells for a significant part of that journey. The broker client should be your champion or cheerleader. Transformation work is too hard to start out with the person hiring you, being the one causing you to doubt yourself and your purpose. If you find yourself in a situation like this, the best thing to do is to try and quickly meet with the power client, otherwise you will end up always on the periphery of the real action and at the mercy of the broker client, who might at times be a gatekeeper to the power client. This means your effectiveness is tied to how the CEO perceives the HR department, and how the HR department perceives you.

Even when you do meet with the power client or CEO, they will often have their own pushback to the transformation process. The **'normal' pushback** that I hear from CEOs includes questions like: "Where has this succeeded before?", "How will this benefit me?", "What will the ROI[17] be for this?", "What will the impact be on the bottom line?" There can certainly be merit to asking such questions, but *how* these questions are asked will tell you the extent to which your power client 'gets it' or not.

Whether I am dealing with broker or power clients, as a black female consultant I often have to go through a whole script where the client questions my approach and the necessity of the exercise of transformation itself. White friends of mine who are also in this business have shared with me that they do not go through the same thing to the extent that I do. When they walk into a meeting, they are just asked to present their plan or strategy. They do get challenged and asked to give a motivation for their approach, but there is a huge contrast to what I typically experience. If you look at this through the lens of unconscious bias, it is understandable why there are many stories about women and black people having to work even harder to convince others that they are competent.

I don't mind being asked questions and being challenged about my approach, but the manner in which the questions are posed can often reveal a lot of hidden biases. Answering someone else's fears is like filling a bottomless hole: no matter what you say, there will always be another question. In such cases it is critical that you state upfront what your conditions of entry are, and to be explicit about how you envision the working partnership. For example, agree on certain important principles like the need to meet personally with the MD, CEO, and Exco very early in the process, as opposed to speaking via the broker client at all times. In this way, the Exco can question the transformation consultant directly rather than constantly working through one person while the intervention is meant for everyone.

I remember one broker client I had. As I was explaining my approach to transformation he interrupted me to say that I wouldn't be listened to in his organisation. He explained that the company didn't rely on government contracts, and that he was not concerned about its B-BBEE rating, and with or without transformation they would still make money. Wondering why they had even called me, I nonetheless continued to explain my company's approach to transformation, but whatever I said he would just criticise, saying things like, "Our CEO will never buy that" etc. What I started to

---

[17] Return on Investment

read was that this guy felt so belittled, his criticisms projected how he was being demeaned within his own company. He had called me in because the company was supposed to transform and he wanted me to come with a magic bullet to fix things, but **there is no magic bullet**. Finally I said it was clear that what I was trying to offer wouldn't work and I wasn't the right person.

Three months later I got a call back from the same person asking me to return, as the company still needed to embark on transformation. I don't know what had happened in between, but when I went in I could see he did not harbour any negative feelings towards me *per se*, but was trying to navigate the dynamics of unconscious bias towards him and by extension towards me as well. Very quickly I realised that this broker client was fearful of presenting a 'black consulting firm' to his CEO. I intuited that he felt our model would demand too much of his executives' time in the firm, and that they would not be able to handle it. Before we got very far I suggested that he let me talk to his Exco directly. I explained that I had nothing to lose in being completely frank and open as an outsider who has a solid model that has been tried and tested.

Eventually, after managing to set up the meeting, I found that the CEO presented the normal challenges of any boss, but agreed to the approach I presented and I ended up signing the client. This unexpected conclusion really highlighted how internalised oppression can blind people with fear, and manifests in such toxic and self-defeating behaviours. The reason I can recognise the behaviours associated with inferiority is that I experienced these feelings myself on many occasions while working in Cape Town.

Having said all that, it is important to share stories of powerful broker clients who have managed to speak truth to power. One such experience is with Nolitha Fakude, who was an executive director at a large oil and gas company headquartered in SA but with business operations across the globe. About 14 years ago, Nolitha invited me to submit a proposal to facilitate diversity dialogue with her Exco Team. She had so much confidence in me and encouraged me all the way. My proposal was approved by the CEO and we co-designed the process that finally worked so well.

This was a time when it was not easy to put forward a black woman consultant to work with a senior executive team without the help of a white 'more trusted' consultant. Up to this day I thank her for standing for what she deemed as right and modelling transformation without any frills or special favours. There are many out there like Nolitha, and it is important to let them know the difference they are making in advancing the transformation agenda and walking the talk, even when it is not easy.

THIS ISSUE OF **ANSWERING PUSHBACK** brings up another subject I must address concerning the way black and women professionals can end up being seen as **custodians of transformation** in their organisations. You know this damaging dynamic is at play when, for example, every time transformation is mentioned, people look at the black member of the team or the lone woman, but when the team is talking about any other topic on finance or other areas of the business, they seem to forget that the person is in the room.

Turning one or a few people into custodians of transformation can poison an organisation's transformation process, particularly for the very people who may have had a passion to drive that process in the first place. This is because when you are viewed as a custodian of transformation, you also become the recipient of the toxins that often come out of the process. If your organisation lacks a sense of collective ownership of its transformation strategy, and by virtue of your colour or gender you are seen as that 'owner' where transformation is seen as 'your problem', then there is little hope for success. And as I have already discussed, if an Exco has not fully bought into the transformation process, you can be sure that many things will go wrong, and all the discomfort and negativity that can come of that will now be projected onto that person or persons.

In other cases, you will see some HR or Transformation Executives being tempted to adopt this 'sole ownership' role, enjoying the illusion that as the 'owners' of transformation they hold some kind of power. While this situation might temporarily serve as a nice ego boost, it is highly unsustainable, as no one person can drive the process of change alone. Either way, the end result will be transformation fatigue, which, as discussed in Chapter 4, can be overpowering and kill the process before any meaningful gains are realised. This will only serve to perpetuate the cycle and lead to comments like, "We knew this thing would not work".

Transformation Work with Multinationals and Expats

IF THERE IS ONE THING I have learned from my experience working in transformation, diversity and inclusion, it is that there is no one-size-fits-all approach. Diversity is all around us, and it manifests in many different ways. That may seem self-evident, but you would be amazed by how limited many people's notion of diversity and inclusion can be, and **expats and multinationals** in South Africa are no exception. When working with expats I have encountered various problems concerning transformation, most of which stem from a general belief that because they are not South African, they should be exempt from concerns about diversity and transformation.

One of the first problems I see occurs when a company has a head office overseas and branches in South Africa, and is unwilling to **customise their diversity and inclusion programmes** to suit the local context. No global diversity programme will work well everywhere. For example, just last year I was invited to help a company with its diversity and inclusion programme, but was told that their headquarters was in Europe and their focus was on gender, so I should not emphasise race in the workshops. They said their global programme was "very carefully designed" by the global office, and I was not to deviate from it. Obviously I was not going to agree to facilitate such a workshop with my knowledge of race issues in South Africa. I advised the client to rather call the workshops gender dialogue sessions, but she insisted that the global headquarters would not agree to even change the name of the workshop. My questions and insistence made her nervous and they opted to not engage my services and we parted ways. I never got to hear what eventually happened, but I have reached a point where it is perfectly fine to lose potential clients because of important principles.

The second problem I often observe is when multinationals fall back on the 'core business' narrative that I have already talked about in earlier chapters. Some expats will tell me that they were not part of South Africa's history, and they don't understand why South Africans are so 'obsessed' with race. I experienced this again recently with one particular client with headquarters in Europe, where workshop participants said, "In this country all you concern yourself with is race. We just want to work". As if we were wasting their time by wanting to deal with these other issues.

I actually used to buy that story, thinking that because they came from a slightly more racially homogenous country and they had more women who were qualified in technical areas, then perhaps they really didn't have that many diversity issues, but then I went to Germany for a different client to facilitate workshops, and saw that this was not true at all. In fact, just last year (in January 2016), the German Ministry of Family introduced quotas for women in the boardrooms to show at least 30% representation. The government saw that for all of their other progressive policies, there was very little female representation at the highest levels, and that without establishing a quota that probably would not change anytime soon. I often think about that example when expats say that South Africa is too focused on numbers.

In Britain, a 2016 report on racial equality released by the Equality and Human Rights Commission showed that black British people are discriminated against in their own country, and that equal work for equal pay is an issue between black and white British nationals. The report went on to say that because government failed to address this issue and instead put it on the back burner, the issue of race is coming back even harder[18]. Yet another example comes from Dubai, where in 2013 they passed legislation ensuring that their own citizens were prioritised for jobs, also a form of B-BBEE.

So expats who say that South Africans are "obsessed" with issues of race and numbers also need to be corrected. South Africans might be more vocal about policies and legislation to correct inequities, and I will be the first to say that fixing only the numbers is never the answer, but ignoring the numbers will only hurt.

For those who say that a deeper solution is needed, I completely agree, which brings me to the third problem I have encountered working with expats. In addition to recognising that transformation work is needed

---

[18] Equality and Human Rights Commission. 2016. *Healing a divided Britain: The need for a comprehensive race equality strategy*. Retrieved from: https://www.equalityhumanrights.com/sites/default/files/healing_a_divided_britain_-_the_need_for_a_comprehensive_race_equality_strategy_final.pdf [Accessed 7 July 2017].

globally, regardless of where you come from, expats working here need to be sensitised to the **importance of cultural nuances**.

If you are an expat in South Africa, even if you do not plan to stay, while you are here you should make an effort to understand how our history impacts our present, and how to speak to people being mindful of those dynamics. For example, some words simply should not be used – I have already talked about my feelings around the use of the term 'non-white', but there are other expressions and ways of talking about the local culture, and it is your responsibility as an expat to learn and to understand. For example, disregarding the impact of South African history and telling people here that we should just 'move on', is so offensive and dismissive of the historical pain that many South Africans still live with. It often baffles me how people so readily acknowledge the deep pain of the Holocaust, but when talking about apartheid, which ended so recently, the same people expect you to 'get over it'. In order to leave the past behind, it must first be acknowledged and never trivialised, regardless of which nation one is talking about. It would be equally wrong for South Africans to say, "The Holocaust happened years ago, so get over it", or talk about the Rwanda genocide with such casual ignorance. Pain is complex and how we process it is different for each individual. I cannot dictate to someone how quickly they need to 'get a life' and move on. That is truly insensitive.

I also need to add here that white superiority is a global problem, so white expats in particular cannot adopt the notion that they are less prone to racism than white South Africans, or are immune from their own unconscious bias or capacity for perpetuating micro-inequities. In the end, **no matter who you are, you cannot say that transformation is none of your business**. Whether you are a leader, manager, or employee, regardless of where you are from or where you live now, you should be part of the process to create an inclusive culture however you can.

INSIGHTS & TIPS

The more I consult on diversity and transformation, the more I see that there is no shortcut to creating an inclusive culture. I have also experienced the significant challenges that still exist for black entrepreneurs, and particularly black female entrepreneurs, to succeed in the South African economy. The process of transformation requires resilience, commitment, and leadership from the front by everyone involved.

The importance of resilience

Overcome feelings of inadequacy

 Practical Tips

- To overcome the long-term effects of feeling inadequate:

    ◦ you must name the problem to overcome it; and

    ◦ you must collect and remind yourself of 'data' that prove otherwise.

- Entry into an organisation or with a new client is the most difficult, especially if you are not from the dominant culture. Being conscious of where the power lies and not catering to the fears of broker or power clients will go a long way in helping you earn your place at the table.

- When offered shortcuts, remember the importance of paying your own way.

- Feel the fear but act anyway.

Unconscious bias in hiring black consultants or engaging with black-owned businesses

People of all races must question their unconscious biases and how these play out professionally

 Practical Tips

- When asked for discounts or favours because a consultant or company is black and/or female-owned, the question should be asked: 'What is happening internally when people do this?'

- It is also important to be conscious of being given piecemeal work with the expectation that you should be grateful for doors that might open. One of the negative consequences of this type of behaviour is that it affects the model or approach you can take, which may result in a lesser product in the end.

- Make sure you have the commitment of the power client. Without this, you should walk away.

Answering other people's assumptions and fears

Deal with perception and don't make assumptions

 Practical Tips

- If you confront perceptions that you are a B-BBEE hire or contracted only for your B-BBEE rating, choose your battles. You know the truth and you can choose whether to challenge this head-on or ignore the perceptions.

- Don't make assumptions about how other people got to where they are: we have all had our hurdles to overcome, and you don't know what someone else has been through if you don't ask.

- When you are making assumptions about someone else's rise to wherever they are, ask yourself why you are invested in creating whatever narrative you have constructed. To what end?

Transformation is everyone's responsibility

Regardless of your nationality or location, commit to transformation

 Practical Tips

- If you are working for or with a multinational, challenge and encourage the leadership to engage meaningfully with these issues. Race and gender biases, as well as other forms of discrimination, are just as present in other countries as they are in South Africa.

- Be sensitive to the pain of South Africa's past and do not tell South Africans to "move on".

- Remember that numbers do matter – don't pretend otherwise.

- Nuances of culture are so important. Take the time to learn the basics wherever you are and respect those differences.

Chapter 9

CREATING A MODEL FOR CULTURE CHANGE

A journey of transformation (2005 - 2017)

If you are building a house and a nail breaks, do you stop
building or do you change the nail?

Rwandan Proverb

MY CLIENT LIST GREW to include companies in financial services, mining,
oil and engineering, among many others. While I was working for these
companies creating transformation plans and running diversity workshops
and trainings, as well as delving deeper into the issues faced by the wide
array of people they employed, I was also addressing international forums
and conferences in North America, Europe, Asia, and other African countries
like Zambia, Namibia and Zimbabwe. Through all of these experiences, the
one constant that has become increasingly clear is that **there is never a
shortcut to creating an inclusive culture.**

Meanwhile, subtle but crucial shifts in terminology were reflecting the
evolution in diversity and transformation thinking. Since its early days, the
way we understood the term 'diversity' had shifted from 'tolerating' diversity
to 'managing' diversity to 'valuing' diversity. In all of these understandings
of diversity, 'diversity' was a thing: a noun describing the differences and
similarities found in any group of people. Over time, the term 'inclusion'
entered the lexicon as the opposite of exclusion. Unlike diversity's charged
but static meaning, inclusion is a 'call to action' that implies that one has to
'do' something for inclusion to take place.

It was when we started seeing how diversity and inclusion work *together*
that a significant semantic breakthrough shifted how we approached the
work of transformation. In other words, we realised the value of inclusion
as a deliberate step taken to acknowledge the way someone's diversity had
caused that person to be actively excluded or simply ignored. By definition,
change requires us to adapt and learn new things: new behaviours, new
thought patterns, new actions, and ultimately, new perceptions and beliefs.
Especially within corporate culture, the burden of change has traditionally
been placed on newcomers or minority groups. With the advent of the idea
of diversity *and* inclusion, however, the responsibility of how diversity should
be managed shifted to *include* everyone.

But how do you bring about that shift? Over the years, I have seen so many diversity efforts that only focused on words, numbers, or targets, or efforts that rushed to implement a weakly formulated strategy, wasting a huge amount of time and money and disappointing those who had hoped for more. Countless individual workshops were held that were well run and meaningful for some participants, but on their own would never realise lasting change. What I saw was that **a systemic approach to culture change was needed**. In other words, everyone in an organisation needed to take responsibility for change; leadership at all levels needed to actively drive and support it, and a clear model that clarified the process across all levels was required.

In response, I developed a **10-step model rooted in direct and active engagement from leadership (see Figure 1)** that is guided by a three-pronged approach. My model relies on the critical interplay between the Head (the 'knowing' or intellectual buy-in), the Heart (the 'being' or emotional buy-in), and the Hands (the 'doing' or visible behaviour change). Although each of the three areas is important – **Head/Knowing, Heart/Being and Hands/Doing** – it is the sum of these three working together that achieves culture change and real transformation.

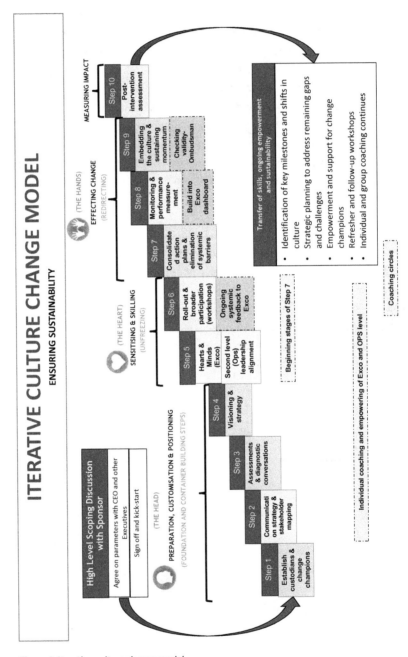

Figure 1: Iterative culture change model

LIKE ANY FUNDAMENTAL SHIFT in an organisation, transformation – or a culture change – will not happen without top leadership's authentic support. My model focuses the transformation process on **activating diversity leadership**, because although working at every level is necessary, without the right leadership, the process will falter.

Given this focus, the first step for an organisational-level transformation journey requires that I sit down with leadership – particularly in scoping conversations with the CEO, Transformation Manager or HR Director, and one or two line-function executives – to establish the parameters of the culture change they want to realise. We start these conversations by identifying who from the highest levels will serve as the transformation programme's sponsor. Ideally that person should be the CEO and/or other executive-level staff.

We go on to use these first sessions to establish a clear understanding of our objectives, and to agree on working definitions for terms like transformation, diversity, inclusion, and culture change. We work through and beyond complicated or academic definitions, while also discarding definitions that emphasise differences. That said, it is important to not swing to the opposite extreme and entertain claims that people do not recognise difference (the 'I don't see colour' fantasy), or pretend that everyone is the same. I also encourage leaders to use this time to familiarise themselves with what diversity means in their local context, for example, we will cover the basics of what the company has already done in the areas of change. Once all this groundwork has been laid with leadership, my model narrows in on the three Hs, which we work through at both the leadership and organisational/ employee levels as outlined below.

The Head: Knowing and Intellectual Buy-In

THE FIRST STEPS ARE ALWAYS those of the **Head, or the intellectual buy-in**. There are many reasons for this, but primarily it is because when challenged with new, uncomfortable, or undesirable things, most people respond best to reason and logic. We start the Head work by establishing a shared vocabulary and discussing the reasons for the change the organisation is being asked to undergo. On some level, most people these days acknowledge that discrimination and exclusion are unfair, illegal, and undesirable behaviours, so we don't waste time with the negatives. You can think of the Head work as preparation, customisation, and positioning. It gives people a **shared foundation of language and reason.**

After agreeing on the transformation vocabulary and reasons for change, we **build a business case for transformation.** We start by **discussing the benefits and opportunities that diversity brings to individuals, groups, organisations, and societies.** During this step, I often find it useful for leaders to sit down with their teams and engage them in identifying what we call the imperatives for diversity and inclusion in their organisation. Leadership would have already gone through this process in earlier sessions, having identified what they see as their imperatives. The primary questions we look at are:

1. *Do we believe transformation is the right thing to do?*

2. *Do we see diversity as a value?*

3. *What are the internal and external benefits for creating an inclusive culture, and what are the risks and liabilities for not acting on this?*

These questions often lead to a combination of robust debate, differences of opinion, and – ultimately and very importantly – recognition that **diverse and inclusive teams are winning teams.** Simply put, when people feel included they want to participate. Looking back at my years at Eskom when business meetings were held in Afrikaans, I distinctly remember how that seemingly small exclusionary practice caused me to lose track of the conversation and get lost in my own thoughts. It definitely impacted how effective I could be. After all, if you have information gaps because of language exclusion, how effective can you really be? In contrast, when people feel recognised and valued for who they are, they are eager to get on with the business at hand. And all of this – plus the advantages of diverse perspectives and worldviews, which I talk about more in Chapter 10 – makes inclusive teams winning teams.

After establishing the logical importance of diversity and inclusion for an organisation, we move on to **ask what exactly is the problem being solved.** That means **diagnosing the issues** in an organisation. This step differs from the first step when we talk about the reason the organisation is being asked to undergo change, in that now we look beyond anecdotal evidence or the opinions of the people who are loudest or closest to leadership, and actually **draw from whatever real data are available**. This often includes administering a survey using electronic and manual questionnaires, collecting quantitative data like recruitment, promotion and retention trends through the lens of demographic variables, as well as recorded employee concerns and experiences.

The final step in the Head work is identifying the ideal end state that the organisation hopes to achieve, and asking what leadership can do differently to achieve this state. In other words, establishing a **clearly defined vision**. One of the vision's most important elements is a clearly stated "Why?" – the driving reason or purpose behind the organisation's commitment to diversity and inclusion. The vision for diversity and inclusion also needs to clearly support the company's broader strategic goals, and place transformation at the centre with other business priorities. If diversity and inclusion are seen as separate from the core business, they will forever be seen as 'nice to have', rather than in any way essential to helping a company realise its value in a manner that shareholders understand.

Fortunately, this is not a hard case to make. Surveys that we have run clearly demonstrate the link between perceptions of unfair treatment, unequal pay scales, and employee dissatisfaction with the disruption of operations, productivity, and delivery. In other words, the 'non-monetary' risks of exclusion and dissatisfaction translate into hard numbers and monetary loss. This link – showing how diversity and inclusion affect broader strategic objectives – should be made very clear in an organisation's Transformation Vision or Statement of Commitment.

The resulting Transformation Vision serves as an invaluable roadmap going forward, reminding leadership and management why diversity and inclusion are vital, and helping to unite the voices, outlooks, and intentions of both leaders and employees.

The Heart: Being and Emotional Buy-In

THROUGHOUT THIS BOOK'S EARLIER CHAPTERS I spoke a lot about the Heart work that underlies the transformation process. The Heart work, or the emotional buy-in, is at the very core of culture change and is the hardest to achieve, both because it is at once so personal and yet often dismissed in the corporate environment as irrelevant or "airy fairy". As such, transitioning from the Head to the Heart can be extremely difficult. This is constantly evidenced in how often you see powerful and well-crafted organisational values hanging on the walls of corporations, posted on company websites, and even quoted by leaders in strategy sessions or at company functions, yet see the opposite in terms of behaviour demonstrated by the same leaders.

From a leadership perspective, the 'being' competence is demonstrated most clearly in **how you as a leader make others feel in your presence**. As my first boss, Yvonne Herring, showed me, the way someone makes you feel is often more about what they do than what they say; it comes from how their body language conveys or withholds acceptance and respect. Without saying a word, I can feel whether a leader accepts me – her energy and presence communicate whether I'm welcome and will be heard. When I ask workshop participants to think of their best or favourite teacher, the answer almost invariably relates to a person who made them feel valued, smart, respected, and/or important. Even those individuals most prone to writing off the value of talking about feelings in the workplace will turn around and use 'feeling' words to describe why they liked their best teachers.

Heart work is about **creating a culture where people feel they belong and are accepted and valued**. People give their best and reach their maximum potential in such a culture. Leaders who can create this kind of environment are often multipliers like my DoL boss, Sipho Pityana. Multipliers create ideal diversity settings by attracting talented people and using them at their highest point of contribution; creating an intense workspace that demands peoples' best, providing opportunities for people to stretch, encouraging debate, and giving others credit for their successes[19]. These all seem like obvious principles of good leadership, but I have found that many leaders struggle to apply them when managing diverse teams. Recognising where the barriers come from in order to overcome them is the basis of Heart work.

Typically, the biggest barriers to the sound management of diverse teams originate in the baggage that we all carry. I have already talked a lot about

---

[19] Wiseman, L. & McKeown, G. 2013. *Multipliers: How the best leaders make everyone smarter.* New York, NY: HarperCollins.

how important it is for anyone on a transformation journey to unzip and work through his or her 'baggage'. This baggage is filled with our early messages about those who are different from us, and our conscious and unconscious biases about these people. All of these things influence our interactions with other people, who are also operating from the starting point of their own baggage. Resistance in moving from the Head to the Heart comes in part because Heart work challenges the core aspects of our identity. When you have been brought up with particular beliefs about your group – be it race, language, sexual orientation, etc. – accepting another possibly divergent view about that group can feel very threatening.

The key work here is recognising that: 1) we all have our individual baggage; 2) we all have certain triggers regarding that baggage; and 3) we all can learn to manage and eventually eliminate those triggers and thus respond differently. The baggage itself will never disappear, but how you respond to it can most certainly change *if you choose to make that effort*. At this stage I have found that some people want to deny that they have baggage – this is the most counter-productive position, as it delays the onset of the inner work that is vital to each person's transformation journey.

Because of the difficulty of this work, leaders must show boldness in challenging their own and others' reluctance to change. This is what I mean when I say leaders must **lead from the front**. Until you do this, the necessary inner work cannot begin – either for you or for the people you are leading. The leader's inner work, like everyone else's, begins with the recognition of his or her 'baggage', and a willingness to sort through and discard things. For example, some of the leaders back at the power stations where I worked at Eskom believed that migrant labourers did not care about their families back home, and that family was therefore 'not important' to black people. While I'm sure most of the leaders who held such a view never thought to question the belief itself or its impact on the workplace, the reality is that those kinds of perceptions fed and justified the discriminatory and even dehumanising treatment of the black people who constituted the majority of the labour force.

The inner work of the Heart requires a constant checking of your assumptions, and by definition does not come naturally. It asks you to question all of your conclusions about 'others' and evaluate how you arrived at them. In other words, to really analyse if they are based on a 'world view' that you have inherited and manufactured, or based on facts that you can verify.

A crucial Heart work tool that we teach people to use is the **underrated but critical competency of listening**. I still remember in his first inaugural speech when Barack Obama said: "I promise to listen to you, especially when we differ." This statement resonated so deeply for me, because it is precisely when we differ that we most need, but generally do not want, to listen to one another. A common example I have witnessed is how during management meetings, if someone brings up a problem around the lack of transformation, rather than being listened to, that person will often be labelled a rebel and reprimanded for not focussing on the 'important' aspects of the business.

People often wrongly assume that listening is about having an answer. In fact, **listening is about being present and dignifying the person speaking with your attention**. You might not know what to do with someone's story, but the fact that you have afforded your time to listen immediately helps reduce their anger or pain. Right there you have already done something. Listening starts with acceptance and a spirit of willingness to hear – this spirit has little to do with what comes out of your mouth.

There are many ways to show that you are willing to listen and to show your intention to be inclusive. Some have nothing to do with 'core business'. For example, asking your employees questions that show an interest in their lives and existence away from the office can go so far in terms of building trust, and **trust is the basis of so many important aspects of working effectively with people**. Once you have established trust through attentive listening, a multitude of other benefits can come through that now-open door. As asserted by Katz and Miller, these include:

- giving each other the benefit of the doubt;
- having expectations to connect and gain something from our interactions;
- listening more attentively and appreciatively;
- looking for the value in what our colleagues say, and building on that;
- showing we are willing to act in spite of discomfort, and trusting our partners to have our backs;

- letting our partners know we have their backs and that they can trust us; and

- creating situations where team members are more likely to extend trust to us[20].

A VERY IMPORTANT PREREQUISITE to effective Heart work is ensuring you have **created a safe space** for people to do this extremely personal, and at times deeply unsettling, work. Without this space, people will switch off. They might be physically present, but they will not engage and learning will not take place. What do I mean by a safe space? When I say, "We're going to have a conversation that's difficult, but you can really express how you feel and not fear a comeback", it needs to be 100% true. The critical thing is that this space is sacred.

The kind of work that can happen in a safe space is seen in an exercise we do call "surfacing the undiscussables". In this exercise we give participants pieces of hexagons-shaped paper to write on, and ask them to identify the undiscussable things – the attitudinal or systemic 'holy cows' – that they feel are preventing or blocking change or transformation in their organisation. Everyone writes anonymously. Then we put the hexagons together to form a honeycomb on the wall, and discuss the issues one by one. Most of the time, 90% of the people present will agree that all the issues are valid. At that point I often share with the participants examples of how other companies have resolved similar issues: forming a committee, benchmarking the issue, or coming up with other ideas to move forward. Very authentic work can happen in this kind of space.

I have also experienced situations where everyone agrees to the rules of the safe space, but in no time, a participant has phoned a manager to say, "So and so has said such and such". I remember a workshop where we were talking about pay scales, and a woman said that as a black woman she was paid less. Her comment got back to a manager, and she was reprimanded and then labelled a rebel from that point onwards. It only has to happen once, and trust is gone forever.

[20] Katz, J.H. & Miller, F.A. 2013. *Opening doors to teamwork and collaboration: 4 keys that change everything*. San Francisco, CA: Berrett-Koehler Publishers, Inc.

As with everything else in this process, **the sanctity of safe spaces comes from leadership**. As a consultant, I sometimes hear when a safe space has been betrayed. I can speak to managers and get them to agree that there won't be victimisation, but they will do what leadership dictates. In places where we have already done workshops with CEOs and they have authentically participated, safe spaces remain sacred. This leads me once again to the importance of the CEO going through the same workshops as employees – it makes a significant difference. If people know their CEO has set aside time for the depth and breadth of inner work, they will follow suit.

Although safe spaces are vital to productive inner work, you also do not want to create a situation where people are so comfortable that no one is challenged to confront their comfort zones. One of my key jobs as a facilitator is to find that delicate balance between creating a safe space for fruitful dialogue and pushing people to go beyond their comfort zones. **Challenging people's comfort zones** is itself a critical tool to deepen discussions, but people must be prepared for what can emerge. We sometimes do an exercise called the 'privilege walk' where people are asked a series of questions concerning diversity status markers, and they move forwards or backwards depending on their responses. For example: "Are you white?" – move one step forward. "Are you gay?" – move one step back. By the end of the exercise, you'll see where different people are standing, and it can open up very fruitful conversations about privilege and unconscious biases.

If there is one topic that attracts discomfort and even anger these days, it is **the topic of privilege**. The mere mention of the words 'white privilege' can conjure up multiple levels of defence in some people. However, if organisations or individuals want to do serious work in diversity and inclusion, white privilege is something that must be acknowledged and broken down. The anger that often emerges in conversations or exercises about privilege is most often a tell-tale sign that you have triggered someone, and ultimately, the issues that trigger people are exactly the things that most need to be addressed. That is what I mean by challenging our comfort zone.

It is through tough and often uncomfortable inner-work that growth and the recognition that we all have baggage emerge. In other words, the recognition that we are all different and similar at the same time. People are often reluctant to talk about their differences for fear of being judged, but when they see how many others have the same issues, or a different set of issues that are no less difficult, it can really render those judgments obsolete.

PEOPLE REVEAL so many surprising beliefs in diversity and inclusion workshops. One thing I am repeatedly shocked by is how many people still believe that the 1994 democratic dispensation was a panacea to all the ills that apartheid left us with. Although South Africa's new Constitution paved the way forward for a just and equal society, the hearts and minds of too many people have yet to reflect what is contained in that document. Statements like "just move on" are still constantly bandied about; as if by 'moving on' the problems of racial inequality will be solved. Instead we need to acknowledge that **race remains fundamentally at the centre of most peoples' reality**.

Despite the fact that diversity includes a multitude of markers, race remains one of, if not the most, emotive aspects of diversity. Thus, while it is true that all diversity markers should be discussed and considered when going through a transformation process, unless you afford race the time and space that it requires, the race dialogue will forever linger. Not only must we afford race the time and space it needs, but we also have to face it head-on. The need for this type of approach makes me think of a National Geographic programme I watched recently showing how lions hunt. The pack puts two male lions in the front while strategically positioning the females around the back and to the sides. When the prey hears the male lions roaring it flees the noise, and in doing so, it runs straight into the jaws of the real danger.

Although it is counterintuitive to confront the loud scary noise, when dealing with the most frightening realities, sometimes the best thing you can do is to go against your flight instinct and rather confront the fear head-on. I often coach leaders in my workshops or one-on-one discussions to refrain from saying things like: "Let's not talk about race", "It's enough about race, let's move on", or "Race is not the only thing in diversity". In the words of Eckhart Tolle, "Whatever you fight, you strengthen, and what you resist, persists".

On a lighter note, I remember a few years ago I was listening to the talk radio programme 702, and the presenter opened by saying that he was tired of talking about race, and how everything turned into politics or racial discussions in South Africa. They had dealt with a heavy topic the day before, and so today's show was about 'walking the dogs'. So what do you think the first caller had to say? "I'm okay with the topic being about walking the dogs, but I just wanted to mention that those dogs bark only at black people." The next caller then insisted on responding to the first caller, and in no time the conversation was back to race.

Jokes aside, this example underscored how if we cannot get away from the subject, let us rather address it consciously and boldly, and keep doing so until it no longer has so much power over us.

The Hands: Doing and Visible Behaviour Change

IF THE HEAD WORK IS ABOUT UNDERSTANDING what diversity and inclusion are and why they are important, and the Heart work is about honestly examining one's baggage and biases so as to change one's responses to issues around diversity and inclusion, the Hands work is where everything comes together in action. The Hands work is the 'doing' – or the visible behaviour change – and demands a total commitment to action and changing the status quo.

In their article, *Inclusion Works*, Ferdman and Deane noted that: "Inclusion is grounded in **what we do** with that diversity when we value and appreciate people because of and not in spite of their differences."[21] Understanding your role and engaging with diversity and inclusion at an emotional level are necessary foundations to change, however what you *do* with this knowledge, particularly if you are in a leadership or management position, is what will ultimately distinguish theory from practice.

In the Hands work, we take all the feedback solicited during the various dialogue sessions with leadership and the analysis of the quantitative data from the diagnostic work, translate them into a **tangible action plan,** and assign responsibility for each action. To start, we outline a high-level implementation plan with the top leadership for creating the desired culture, including clear mandates and guidelines for decision-makers at all levels. I always recommend a structured approach to creating a culture of inclusion.

---

[21] Ferdman, B.M. & Deane, B.R. (eds.). 2014. *Diversity at work: The practice of inclusion.* San Francisco, CA: Jossey–Bass.

This structured approach outlines the different roles that all management levels need to engage in. This means clearly identifying problem areas, and the different 'calls to action' that management will actively adopt to attend to those problems. A roadmap to implementation is so important to the long-term success and sustainability of your transformation process. The roadmap should include a strategic action plan addressing two areas necessary for effective change and creating an inclusive culture. These are attitudinal change and systemic change.

Attitudinal change means addressing the personal and collective baggage present in your organisation. This process requires what we call diversity and inclusion sensitisation, which takes the form of multiple interventions at both the intra-personal (i.e. the personal work that each individual has to do, as in Gandhi's famous quote "Be the change that you want to see in the world") and interpersonal levels (i.e. interactions with other individuals or teams). The strategic action plan for attitudinal change should address the Heart work to be done at the employee levels, and more deeply at the leadership levels. The latter would include things like carefully designed small group sensitisation sessions and workshops for leaders and management to equip them with practical skills to deal with stereotypes, biases, and discrimination in their teams, as well as to help them create high performance teams where everyone feels heard, understood, and included.

Meanwhile, all the dialogue sessions and every intervention should contain a clear answer to the question of "Why are we doing this?" If you do not explain the 'Why?' of any intervention, people will always externalise the reasons they are embarking on a project or exercise (e.g. the law demands that we do this). For example, I recently worked with a leadership team that had not spent enough time interrogating the question of why their company must transform. When I referred them to the preamble of the Constitution, where there is a clear case for change and transformation in South Africa, the Managing Director said, "Wow, I never knew that this was so clearly outlined in the Constitution". My own assumption (yes, I do still hold assumptions and reach conclusions too quickly myself!) was that senior executives who are tasked with leading change and transformation in their companies would at least be familiar with the preamble to the South African Constitution, but I was shown that this is not always the case. This is what I mean by always ensuring that the 'Why?' is clear to all parties at all stages. Understanding the

'Why?' helps participants understand and feel how integral this work is for building effective teams and achieving organisational goals and objectives.

While attitudinal change interventions help us to deal with exclusion, unfairness, and discrimination at the intra-personal and inter-personal levels, we must also examine how those things are embedded in an organisation's policies, systems, and procedures. **Systemic change** refers to the interventions needed at the systemic or structural level. I have found that addressing exclusion at a systemic level means looking at every step of an employee life cycle and implementing changes in each stage. Leaders should start by asking what systemic barriers are blocking inclusive leadership, for example the EE Act states that an exercise of equal work for equal pay must be embarked upon in companies where pay parity is ensured. If two employees work in the same department reporting to the same manager and operating under the same 'job family' (meaning doing the same job), but one employee is paid 30% more in basic pay than the other, this a clear demonstration of systemic discrimination, and systemic discrimination fundamentally undermines even the best attitudinal work. Meaning that even if I have gone through great interpersonal dialogue sessions and respect my colleague, if I then discover that he is paid more than me for doing the same job, it does not matter how well we have done our interpersonal work, I will now struggle to relate to him because I feel the system favours him. Throughout my work I have discovered that systemic unfairness is found in many workplace practices, such as:

- How and where positions are advertised.

- Who forms part of the recruitment panel.

- How appointments are made.

- How tasks, projects and responsibilities are allocated.

- How performance discussions are held and ratings allocated.

- Promotion decisions and succession planning.

- Team meetings (who is invited, who is listened to, who leads, who is overlooked).

IT IS IMPORTANT THAT leadership recognises that the 'doing' is not only found in big, obvious changes, but also in smaller engagements and interactions. We call these smaller actions **micro-messages and micro-affirmations** (as opposed to micro-aggressions). For example, I worked with a CEO who discovered through our process that his employees felt one of the organisation's biggest problems was that top leadership was totally inaccessible and unaware of what they were dealing with on a daily basis. In response, the CEO did two things. First he started a blog, which gave him a direct line of communication to employees, inviting them to engage and promising that he would come back to them within 48 hours on any issues they raised. He promised that if he could resolve the issue on the blog, he would do so, and if he could not, he would refer them to right person. The first two months the volume on the blog was so high that he ended up assigning a team to help him sift through the posts and keep his promise of responding within 48 hours. However, by month four or five, the volume of queries had dropped radically and he was able to keep up with it mostly on his own. His employees had been testing him to see how interested he really was. But employees are fair – they understood that the CEO couldn't answer every question – and once they saw that he was willing to try, that made a tremendous difference. The second thing he did was to start his own unannounced 'walkabouts', where he would literally walk around the offices, coming over and asking people if he could sit with them for a few minutes. He'd often just ask about their kids, or had they seen the cricket game the other day. Employees really valued this connection, and felt he was honouring them as people. Suddenly they felt that leadership was accessible. There were such amazing benefits from him doing these two relatively small things.

HOW CAN THE HEAD, HEART AND HANDS WORK TOGETHER to create a sustainable and inclusive workplace? Since the Head represents intellectual buy-in, it is important to begin there. This is where visions, targets, and plans belong. If a management team had formulated a Vision for Diversity and Inclusion (or in some instances a broader Transformation Vision), these are captured in a strategic planning document. But this is exactly what they are – statements and targets in a document or spreadsheet. I have never seen a spreadsheet transform an organisation. Many people think that by virtue of developing a transformation plan with stretch targets and a vision they will transform, but this is not the case; something else is needed to progress beyond numbers.

That something else is the Heart work. The Heart work that follows is the work of inclusion. How should you 'be' as a leader for this strategy document to be taken seriously? How do you as a leader talk about transformation? How do you talk about diversity? Do you always refer to it as a 'burdensome' exercise that stands in the way of real business? If that is the case (which it so often can be, even at the executive leadership level), then the targets and plans contained in your strategy document will never be more than spreadsheets, because employees look up to their leaders and will soon detect that the plans and numbers are devoid of meaning.

But when leaders make an effort to engage their own hearts – even bringing on coaches to help them grapple with the concepts of introspection, unconscious bias, and how to allow themselves to be vulnerable – they lead transformation efforts with authenticity. In such cases, a company will make significant progress with diversity and inclusion because, again, employees look up to their leaders for cues, and seeing a genuine effort, they will follow. Once a leader has engaged the Heart and shown others the way, the work of the Hands, or the implementation, comes naturally.

INSIGHTS
& TIPS

The field of transformation or change is often accused of being "airy-fairy" with no trackable measures. The iterative model that I have developed provides for tangible tracking, and pre- and post-assessments. At the same time, our approach ensures that companies deal holistically deal with the Head, Heart, and Hands competencies.

Many of our clients who have followed our recommended model attest to a real shift in the culture as a result of following the steps. Organisations, especially large organisations with offices spread across different cities or provinces, find this model particularly useful because of its clear structure. Line managers like knowing that the process of transformation or change that the company is adopting hangs on something, and is guided by a tried and tested model. It also provides an opportunity for any business unit leader sitting in whatever location to know where they are in the model, and in their journey as an organisation.

Unlike some change initiatives that are unguided and lack milestones, each of the 10 steps in our model has something to show in terms of achievements or outcomes, and leads to a sense of real achievement for leadership and employees alike.

The Head

Key "knowing" competencies:

- Willingness to broaden your understanding of diversity and inclusion.
- Willingness to listen and engage in continuous dialogue and learning.
- Desire to know why diversity and inclusion are important for your organisation, and willingness to take the risks that leadership demands.
- Ability to identify the business case for diversity with both tangible and intangible benefits and risks.
- Ability to take responsibility for educating yourself about your own and other's experiences of diversity and inclusion or exclusion.
- Knowing where you are going and how you would like to get there; developing the Diversity and Inclusion Vision.

Developing a Diversity and Inclusion Vision and Strategy: Some core questions to ask when developing this strategy include:

- What is your ideal end state with regard to diversity and inclusion?
- What is your big picture or aspiration with regard to diversity and inclusion?
- Does your organisation recognise diversity and inclusion as part of their competency evaluation when selecting leaders?
- How do leaders learn to lead inclusively without losing focus of the purpose and fundamental mandate of the organisation?

The Heart

We talk about Heart work and the competence of 'being', but how should successful, inclusive, 21st century leaders *be*? How must they 'show up' in the workplace? Based on my years of experience in the field, the key to inclusive leadership skills lies in continuous learning through engaging in dialogue with an open mind and an understanding that vulnerability is not a weakness, but a means towards a useful end.

Moving the Hands

Engage in the ongoing work of transformation through implementing attitudinal and systemic changes

 Practical Tips

- Ask yourself a range of question to test whether you are putting Head and Heart knowledge into action:

    ○ **Do I solicit opinions?** Do I find opportunities to ask, "I'd like your opinion about..."?

    ○ **Do I connect on a personal level?** Do I take a few minutes to engage in a non-business conversation with a colleague?

    ○ **Do I ask open questions?** When I have a negative reaction to a colleague's statement or suggestion, do I lead my response with a question, not a statement?

    ○ **Do I attribute/credit ideas?** Do I acknowledge, by name, the 'owner' of an idea in a meeting?

    ○ **Do I monitor facial expressions and body language?** Am I conscious of my facial expressions and body language while listening?

    ○ **Do I actively listen?** Am I attentive to the speaker in order to enhance the quality of their message, or do I frequently interrupt or cut them off?

    ○ **Do I draw in participation?** When addressing a group, do I actively encourage participation from everyone?

    ○ **Do I monitor personal greetings?** Am I aware of who I greet and who I don't greet?

    ○ **Do I respond constructively to differences?** When responding to someone's comment with which I disagree, do I show that I understand their perspective before I offer a different view?

- Develop a bias for action around issues of diversity and inclusion.

- Expect tension and conflict and learn to manage it as you implement change.

- Use language and behaviour that is non-biased and inclusive.

- Work collectively with others and support efforts that combat prejudice, harassment, discrimination, exclusion, and oppression in all its forms.

- Use your rank and privilege as a leader to address micro-messaging and micro-aggressions.

Chapter 10

BOLD, VALUES-DRIVEN AND CONSISTENT

How to Lead from the Front

An army of sheep led by a lion can defeat an army of
lions led by a sheep.

Ugandan Proverb

LEADERS DETERMINE A COMPANY'S CULTURE, and as Richard Barrett
discusses in his book, *Liberating the Corporate Soul*[22], culture has become
a source of competitive advantage. Since all companies aim to access
and retain the best talent, they indirectly compete in the realm of culture.
Meanwhile inclusive cultures themselves are naturally more competitive
and dynamic, because they require everyone to stretch. By intentionally
recruiting a more diverse array of people, a company knowingly creates
a situation that calls for 'business unusual'. This means that if you have
been a supervisor leading a relatively homogenous group of employees for
many years – people who share similarities in language, culture, traditions,
practices etc. – and your organisation is now intentionally recruiting
employees who differ in terms of race, gender, age, etc., this represents
a new challenge for management and staff alike. Leading or supervising a
diverse team will require something different – something more. So now is
the time to ask yourself, **what should I as a leader be doing to improve and
evolve**?

To start, CEOs need to question how far they are willing to go – and how
far along they are – in their personal transformation journey. Executive
managers should be asking what inclusion means in their departments, and
how well their departments reflect the transformation vision of the overall
organisation. **Self-introspection** is key, but honest feedback from the people
you work with is also vital. When **inviting feedback**, you must do so in such a
way that makes people believe you actually want to improve or change your
behaviour. I remember a manager I worked with who literally pounded the
table while saying, "I want everyone to give me feedback". He was surprised
when people said nothing. I had to explain that the way he asked for
feedback made people wonder what he would do with them if they replied
honestly. So asking people how you come across to them is valuable,

---

[22] Barrett, R. 1998. *Liberating the corporate soul: Building a visionary organization*. Woburn, MA:
Butterworth Heinemann.

but only if you do so with openness and an intention to act positively on the feedback you receive.

A leader's willingness to fully engage in the transformation process – do the inner work, lead from the front, participate in the same types of workshops and trainings that employees do, and solicit and respond to honest feedback – sometimes also means **being open to the need to step away**. As a facilitator, there are times when I can see that no one in a group is talking because they are defaulting to seniority – this can mean a few people or even just one key person. You can see how the group relates to a particular person in the room; how before agreeing on anything they will check to see if that person's head is nodding yes or no. As a facilitator, this tells me that the group is not safe to step fully into vulnerability, and if I encourage them to do so, I might actually cause damage.

I remember speaking to a focus group about the culture operating in their division. Although I could see quite a few people were fearful and hesitant, one employee spoke up openly. About two weeks after that focus group session I received a call from another participant, informing me that the employee who had spoken up was being victimised for haven spoken so honestly in front of the boss. This employee was apparently so traumatised that he was contemplating leaving the company. I tried to track him down, but he did not want to engage further. This experience underscored for me my personal responsibility in leading people to voice their opinions. Even though I had received an assurance from senior management that honest, robust conversation was what they wanted, I discovered later that it was not safe to do so.

Since then I have become cautious about leading a group into vulnerability if I can see any signs that it won't be safe. For example, I later found myself in a workshop where I could see the group continually deferring to a manager; I observed the group body language and saw fear. During the tea break I told the manager what I had seen and asked if he would leave. He agreed and once he was gone, people really opened up. In this instance, the complaints were not about him personally but about others who were perceived to be close to him, so his departure from the room helped surface issues.

In some cases, the way a senior person's presence blocks progress is more obvious. Some leaders can be very domineering – how they speak, cutting people off, putting people down, etc. It does not even necessarily have to be a case of seniority – some people are just more vocal or overbearing. In these cases I prefer to sort the person out nicely but publicly, because this kind of behaviour is something a person should be conscious of. I once did a workshop with the Johannesburg High Court and one judge just wouldn't stop talking. With some humour I told everyone that I was going to set a quota on how many words each person could say, adding that our workshop wouldn't be very useful if we only heard certain voices. The judge knew exactly what I was doing and even laughed about it.

The value of humility and abundance

HUMILITY IS A QUALITY COMMON TO MANY TRULY GREAT LEADERS, and is probably a prerequisite to great *inclusive* leadership. There is a model I like to use to illustrate the relationship between humility, competence, and effectiveness, called the '**stages of competence**'. At the lowest level you have unconscious incompetence, which is followed by conscious incompetence and then conscious competence. At the highest level is unconscious competence. An example that captures these stages is that of a child learning to ride a bike. At the first stage he doesn't know what he doesn't know – he doesn't even know what a bike is, never mind his own inability to ride one. Then he starts to realise that there is this thing that is riding a bike, but he can't do it. Then he starts to learn to ride, but he has to think about it all the time. And finally he rides effortlessly – the skill becomes second nature.

For leaders on a transformation journey, the ideal is to function at Level 4, that is, where you are unconscious of what you know about diversity and inclusion – where knowledge has translated to wisdom – because this is the level where your influence on others is greatest. The leaders who are the most problematic are those who get stuck at Level 3: they know what they know, and they want everyone else to know what they know too. Related to this is a need to cut others down for what they do not know. People at this stage struggle to be multipliers because they are too busy proving themselves or discrediting others. Leaders like this often need to be taught to understand the impact their behaviour can have on people who look up to them; how a casual remark or thoughtless act can set an enthusiastic young professional back miles.

I remember doing a survey for a company whose marketing manager had called us in for their presentation of the results. She had decided to give a talented young man exposure by letting him present to the Exco team. This young man came in with his laptop, but had compatibility issues when trying to connect to the projector. The moment the trouble started the CEO looked pointedly from his watch to the young man. You could feel the tension rising. The marketing manager apologised and went to find someone from IT. As she was leaving, the CEO said, "Tell your guy 15 minutes is already gone". I could literally see that young man perspiring and shaking. I felt terrible, but as a visitor I could do nothing. Finally the marketing manager returned with an IT person and sorted out the laptop. The CEO then told the young man, "You have three minutes". You can imagine how the presentation went. The young man was finished before he could even speak. The CEO then smacked the desk and said, "That's it, it's over", and got up and left. I sat there marvelling at his inability to just say something like, "Don't worry, it happens to all of us". Because it does.

I kept thinking about that young man, and how much work it may take for him to rebuild his confidence and get past that experience. There is so much that a drop of humility can do to make someone else's life easier. I constantly see how leaders underestimate the power and influence that comes with the privilege they hold. The question is, what type of leader will you choose to be?

WHEN TALKING ABOUT INCLUSIVE AND HUMBLE LEADERS, those who have met him all have a Madiba story to share, so here is mine. Around 1995, when I was working at Eskom, I was invited to Mr Mandela's house for dinner. His spokesperson was getting married and his fiancé, who reported to me at Eskom, had invited me to come and to bring a friend. We were told on a Tuesday that dinner would be on Saturday. I learned that there would only be four of us present, which made me nervous – had it been a large event I could have relaxed. In the days leading up to the dinner I was anxious: how would I impress Nelson Mandela? I obsessively read most newspapers that had something on world politics, international relations and the South

African economy that week, wanting to be sure I would sound 'intelligent'. Ah – did I waste my time!

The dinner turned out to be a relaxed and 'no frills' event. Mr Mandela mostly talked about Qunu, the village he came from, telling stories like the time he had to mediate a conflict between neighbours, and how he enjoyed walking among villagers chatting to them about the ordinary events of their daily lives. Then he asked about us, giving each of us the platform to shine. He had this way of disappearing into the background of a conversation while engaging you in a manner that allowed your natural genius to blossom. I never forgot that.

I heard many other similar stories of him from other people – how he would insist on thanking the chef personally, or greet security guards by name and ask how their families were doing. He was a person who knew what he had, and as a result could give it to others.

It was a lesson I first learned from my mother, but one that I saw repeatedly in all the best leaders I have had the pleasure of knowing: **a spirit of care and abundance leaves a lasting impression**, and you will always get back what you give. It is so important for people in positions of power and privilege to act with humility and abundance, and to seek opportunities to uplift others. If I have a candle and light 100 other candles, my light is strengthened, not diminished. Again, this leads back to my earlier point about how a leader makes you feel in their presence. I think of Maya Angelou's quote about how people won't remember what you know or say, but they will remember how you made them feel. Those leaders who make other people feel special and show them that they matter leave great legacies. Leaders with an abundance mentality catalyse those around them to be more innovative and creative, and to perform at their very best.

The Evolution of Diversity and Inclusion

AS LEADERS GROW, so the work of diversity and inclusion has also evolved. As I discussed in Chapter 9, the way we have thought about diversity has changed over the years, from a buzzword in the phrase 'value in diversity', to an asset to be managed. Despite these subtle shifts in how we think about diversity, a stubborn constant remains, i.e. the way managers too often treat diversity as a number or target for recruitment. While they may not see it, to others it is very clear that a department as diverse as a rainbow can still exclude people. In other words, diversity in a team does not in itself translate into an asset. Ideally, this realisation should bring leaders to the new understanding that diversity presents a world of options, but is only an asset if you *do* something with it. That is where inclusion comes in as the key to unlocking the potential of diversity and getting the best out of everyone.

A shift into the language of inclusion is an important one, because diversity is actually easy: as soon as you have more than one person in a room – they can both be 50-year-old white males with greying hair, but one is divorced and one is married – you have diversity. Even when you have the broadest range of diversity markers present in a group, diversity still just *is*. But inclusion is a call to action that acknowledges that things don't just happen automatically, *people* have to make it happen. As such, **the call to action of inclusion operates at three levels**.

The first level of the call to action speaks to leaders. Leaders should be modelling inclusive behaviour, actively looking for exclusion in their organisations, and alert to the not so obvious types of exclusion. The second call to action speaks to those who are excluded: you must speak up and include yourself. As someone who is excluded you must recognise that others on your team may be clueless about what you are experiencing. Even if it does not mean anything will necessarily change or happen right away, speaking up means you know you have raised the issue and you have seized your own responsibility in the process. The third call to action is to the observers: those who are not being excluded or doing the excluding, but through the power of proximity and position can also do something about it.

In the end, inclusion is a call to action for everyone in an organisation to be an activist, because creating an inclusive culture does not just benefit those being excluded, it is actually a way for everyone to affirm the desire to work in an environment of fairness and justice.

The problem of implementation

THROUGHOUT ALL THE STAGES and iterations of our ideas of what diversity and inclusion are, and how we transform to change culture, a constant remains: this task will never be finished or easy. These days our focus in transformation work has moved to proper implementation. When we talk about proper implementation it is useful to go back to the legislation – in particular South Africa's Employment Equity Act, which has been so misinterpreted in the past. A lot of the criticism concerning transformation is based on perceptions that the Employment Equity Act and/or B-BBEE legislation is flawed and has allowed people who are not qualified to get jobs – all those narratives about merit and blackness and competence that I have already talked about.

My response to the negative narratives about EE and merit is that the problem is not with the legislation, but rather with its implementation. So many of the problems in transformation are the result of people ticking boxes to 'get the numbers' without engaging in the hard but vital corollary work of culture change. It is essential that issues of implementation are not allowed to obscure the value and necessity of the legislation itself, or the value and necessity of the robust transformation processes that some organisations have managed to undertake. So what are some of the biggest **problems of implementation** and what can we do about them?

The first and most common problem I have seen is the **failure of companies to act on what they have committed to** in their transformation plans. In these cases, I mostly hear managers say they are not transforming because they cannot fire white people and replace them with black people[23], yet when a vacancy comes up either due to natural attrition or a resignation, the same managers fail to take advantage of the opportunity to employ a black person and ensure an equitable workplace. Instead they employ a white person and talk about the need to hire based on merit. It is important to acknowledge the real challenge of finding certain skills among previously disadvantaged groups, but leaders too often use this challenge as an excuse without trying hard enough to implement their agreed-upon plans. Unwillingness to do the work to find appropriate diversity hires sits at the source of a lot of mistrust and conflict, which then linger in an organisation and further block culture change.

---

[23] The Labour Relations Act, which protects the rights of all employees regardless of colour or creed, also prevents a company from unilaterally firing white people only to employ black people.

Some of my recommendations for companies struggling in this area include the need to look closely at the approach taken by the recruitment agencies that they rely on – are these recruitment agencies themselves diverse and/or committed to diversity? Are they biased against certain types of candidates? Companies must also look at their strategies for recruiting graduates – do they have an unconscious bias against certain universities and therefore rule out the opportunity to source excellent and diverse graduates from those institutions? Is the company involved in skills development at a school level to build a future pipeline of critical skills? These, and many others, are the types of questions organisations must ask themselves.

The second most common problem of implementation is very much related to the first, and is when **senior leadership does not walk the talk** – meaning they are not willing to do the Heart work and boldly lead from the front in the manner demanded for true culture change to occur. I often see this in the form of senior leaders remaining silent in response to managers who are vocal in their opposition to transformation and the strategy that has been agreed upon. When this happens, you know you've lost your transformation process.

Another manifestation of this is when leadership rewards managers who are not making progress on transformation. For example, many managers are good in a technical area (e.g. finance or operations), but bad at managing a diverse staff and/or creating an inclusive climate that is conducive to making all employees excel. In too many instances such managers are rewarded for their good technical work, and may even be seen receiving leadership awards. If those same managers are accused of racism or sexism, such complaints are often ignored because the manager is considered 'good' for the company, and there is a reluctance to confront his/her behaviour. But being good at a technical level does not mean the manager is good at addressing the Heart issues that are also important to an organisation's transformation and therefore long-term success. By rewarding a manager like this, you are clearly conveying the relative (un)importance of your company's stated transformation goals.

SO HOW DO WE ADDRESS THESE THINGS? As I've said already, culture change requires commitment, resilience and leading from the front. And it should come as no surprise that all of these problems usually originate with senior leadership failing to allocate the necessary time, resources, and personal commitment to understand and do the work of the Heart, or to bring about the culture change that their organisations need. Therefore, the solutions lie with leadership.

The first non-negotiable is that **all leaders should have coaches**, and in fact there should be coaching at all levels if possible. If a manager is entrusted with the responsibility of managing others, having a personal coach should not be regarded as a luxury but as a requirement of responsible leadership. In other words, coaching should not be a 'nice to have', but a given in any organisation that is serious about transformation.

Another thing leadership can do is **link peoples' bonuses to achievements in transformation**. If organisations can link bonuses to sales targets, why can't they link them to transformation targets?

Finally, there should be consequences when people actively resist transformation. Senior leaders must know that in order to create an atmosphere of trust, difficult decisions need to be taken. **Decisive leadership and consistency** are two of the most important ingredients of trust. If there is a supervisor who is known to all senior leaders as someone openly resisting change, allowing that person to carry on – and even rewarding that person for other things – creates a serious trust deficit in the organisation's culture. Lack of trust will impact any other transformation commitments that the same leadership team might want to make. In the end, decisive action that is seen by all will go a long way in proving that transformation is taken seriously.

Poor performance and tokenism

ONE OF THE HUGE ELEPHANTS in the transformation room is the issue of poor performance and tokenism. If you as a manager think that someone is performing poorly, the worst disservice you can do to transformation is to not call poor performance by its name because the person involved is black, female, etc., and you fear being called racist for attending to it. It is your role as a manager to be brave enough to speak up when you see poor performance, but the key is to **act with consistency, confidence, and fairness**. In other words, be very sure that you are not only looking for poor performance in black people, and that your own unconscious bias is not affecting how you implement policies and evaluations.

Consistency and fairness are the best policies for managing performance. Sometimes you need to look for the signals that tell you something untoward is going on. One of my clients conducted an exercise where she analysed ratings given to all employees over a three-year period. She discovered that in terms of racial profiles, black employees consistently received the lowest ratings. She commissioned an in-depth examination, which found no logical basis for the trend. Given that there is nothing inherent about the performance of any race group, the emergence of this trend was a signal to search deeper for hidden bias in how performance reviews were conducted. This particular client was able to change the situation moving forward because she did her homework, named the problem, and then dealt with it.

Fair and consistent application of policies and systems also gives one the credibility and confidence to deal with poor performance across the board, without fear of being labelled as either racist or overly lenient with any particular group. If you see someone continually struggling, you can judge if it is a struggle of attitude or of competence, and you can do something about it based on evidence. Say you have noticed a performance problem with a black employee whom you have managed and evaluated over the course of several quarters. If you approach that employee the same way you approach a white employee, and say, "I've noticed these problems in your performance and I want to help you", and that person shouts racism, it is fine as long as you can say, "Okay, if you think I'm being racist then follow the grievance procedure". If you have your evidence, it's really about staying your ground as a manager.

But because unconscious bias is just that – unconscious – you must also be willing to listen to feedback about your own behaviour as a manager or leader. If an employee thinks you are being racist, it is important for you as a manager to be willing to say, "This is my evidence about where you didn't perform, but show me where you think I'm being unfair, show me where you think I might be unconsciously biased". And then allow the employee to tell you.

This is where the listening comes in. Listen well. The person might fabricate a story – people are people after all – but they might point something out that you were unaware of, and if so, you have now learned something. But you have to be open and sufficiently self-aware to hear about and acknowledge your own possible bias and how it may have coloured your evaluation or perceptions. All of this links back to why all leaders and managers should have access to coaches, because these situations are not always black and white.

Dealing with poor performance and fear of discrimination requires being firm and consistent with all your employees, but it also requires openness in confronting your own unconscious bias, because that may also be playing a role.

If you are the person being accused of poor performance and you think it is race related, you also have a responsibility to check your own possible biases and prove that what has happened really is discrimination. You may also want to first consult with your coach or a trusted mentor. You can't just shout discrimination and leave it there; you need evidence that shows that your manager is unfairly applying policies to you because of some kind of discrimination.

The point is that both the manager and the employee potentially being discriminated against have responsibilities in this situation, and working through these things and listening to one another on an ongoing basis is how you work together to change your environment. That is exactly what culture change is: an ongoing and challenging process that requires listening and honest self-reflection, but ultimately yields great rewards.

Activating Diversity: the tangible benefits

THROUGHOUT OUR WORK to create culture change, we must not forget that leaders and managers have responsibilities to lead their organisations towards certain goals that do not appear to be connected to transformation, and are constantly navigating a multitude of pressures just to get through the day. Although I might have ideals about creating a more fair or inclusive world, I also need to accept without judgment that activism is not everyone's calling or even interest. That said, one of the big lessons I have seen proven so many times is that people in inclusive cultures are better at responding to daily pressures and finding new and creative ways to achieve an organisation's goals.

In other words, **inclusive cultures are better cultures**, insofar as they are cultures where people innovate, cooperate, trust, and give of themselves. What companies need to understand and be reminded of is that diversity and inclusion is an asset to business because it taps into diversity of personality and thought. There are so many kinds of personalities and ways of thinking, and teams benefit from that diversity. Allowing for and encouraging diversity and inclusion thus spark different ways of thinking, and different ways of thinking can have tangible benefits for teams and organisations.

A US study[22] compared juries made up of homogenous versus diverse teams of jurors. In contrast to the homogenous teams that reached decisions quickly, they found that the diverse teams took longer but were more thorough in their deliberations. The study's conclusion was that if on your team you have different worldviews – so perhaps a black person, a Chinese-American person, a Jewish person, etc. – everyone will ask questions from his or her different perspective, drawing attention to cultural nuances that others would not necessarily see. In short, our **cultural differences are an asset**. Yes, the process might take longer, but the outcome is of a higher quality.

Something we need much more of here in South Africa is documentation of the many cases where the thinking from diverse teams has positively impacted a company's bottom line, because diversity is known to spur innovation. People innovate from the basis of who they are, so different backgrounds and cultures lead to different approaches to innovation. To this end, an inclusive culture can be a powerful form of competitive advantage.

This was demonstrated in the case of Vodacom employee Nkosana Makate's multi-billion rand 'Please Call Me' concept. Makate said the idea came to him after yet another fight with his girlfriend, who claimed he wasn't calling her due to a lack of airtime. We need to document and elevate cases studies

---

[24] Sommers, S.R. (2006). On racial diversity and group decision-making: Identifying multiple effects of racial composition on jury deliberations. *Journal of Personality and Social Psychology, 90*, 597.

such as these, which demonstrate the value of diversity in corporate teams, and then present them at business schools.

In the end, whether an organisation changes culture to become more inclusive because of idealistic or pragmatic principles, the result is that your employees will be more satisfied and more trusting, and will give more to the organisation. That said, when organisations attempt to implement transformation programmes for purely pragmatic reasons, the results will likely disappoint, because the hard truth in transformation remains.

INSIGHTS & TIPS

In my experience working with leaders, I have seen time and again how they and their leadership styles determine a company's culture, and in turn how a company's culture determines its competitive advantage and profitability.

Building Cultural Capital

Intentional and consistent attitudes and behaviours are required to build an inclusive culture

 Practical Tips

- Take time for regular self-introspection: what are you doing as a leader to ensure inclusivity in your organisation?

- Invite feedback on how others feel in your presence and what impact you are having in the areas of transformation and inclusion.

- Know when to withdraw as a leader to give others space to air their views without fear of victimisation. However, importantly, work towards the skill of being able to create safe spaces where your presence is not threatening and where there is trust that you will not break the confidentiality of what is shared.

- In the spirit of humility and abundance, share what you know wherever you are and understand that by giving, nothing is taken away from you.

- Strive to be a Level 4 leader: one who is not self-conscious or overly proud about what he knows because that knowledge has translated into wisdom.

A Call to Action

Remember that diversity and inclusion is a call to action

 ## Practical Tips

- Ensure that your approach to diversity and inclusion is activated at three levels:

  o For leadership: be alert, be aware and be looking for instances of exclusion that need to be corrected.

  o For those who feel excluded: speak up and take responsibility for raising your concerns.

  o For observers who neither feel excluded nor are doing the excluding: use proximity and power to push for the inclusion of those being excluded. Refuse to be a bystander.

- Ensure that your organisation follows through on its transformation plans.

- Ensure that managers truly understand their roles with regard to implementing the EE Act and other important pieces of labour legislation.

- Do not allow known transformation resistors to be rewarded for other aspects of work.

- Link bonuses to transformation targets.

No one walks this journey alone

Put systems and support structures in place to ensure support during the transformation journey

Practical Tips

- Agree as a leadership team that everyone needs coaching, mentoring and assistance to overcome unconscious biases and to do the hard, inner work. This means the following:

  ◦ Provide personal coaching for leaders.

  ◦ Provide bridging programmes.

  ◦ Implement accelerated development programmes.

  ◦ Make sure transformation committees are relevant with visible support from top leadership.

Ensuring proper implementation and a strong business case

Refuse to fall into the trap of misapplying the legislation or using easy excuses to not transform; demonstrate that transformation is good for business.

 Practical Tips

- Ensure the consistent application of policies and procedures by calling out poor performance whenever you see it: do so fairly, consistently, and with evidence. Also, be aware of the possibility of unconscious biases and how they can influence the way you see performance.

- People who feel they are being unfairly evaluated must also question their own biases and bring evidence to the table.

- Do the hard work of finding appropriate diversity hires. This may require creative thinking and tough conversations, but it will be a competitive advantage for your organisation.

- Elevate case studies that demonstrate how diverse teams help the bottom line, and use these examples to promote transformation in your organisation and in our broader society.

Chapter 11

MY DUAL ROLE AS FACILITATOR AND SUBJECT OF DISCRIMINATION

Directing and Acting in the Same Movie

Hope does not kill, I shall live in hope of getting
what I seek another day.

South African saying

I OFTEN COMPARE the experience of being a black female facilitator for
diversity and inclusion to what I imagine it's like acting in a film that you are
also directing. I am guiding other people on how to lead inclusively or how
to deal with exclusion or discrimination, but also experiencing discrimination
and doing my own inner work at the same time.

I remember a workshop where we were discussing meritocracy and race,
and things had become quite heated. I finally explained how the definition of
the word 'meritocracy' itself is straightforward, but despite the word having
no underlying racial associations, people have attached a racial connotation
to it, reflecting a belief that only white people can be appointed on merit.
A silence fell over the room. Most of the white participants kept glancing at
my white co-facilitator. You could feel the weight of the crowd's desire that
he say something. As I was about to go on to another point, one participant
gathered his courage and looked at my colleague and said: "Is that really
true? Do you also find that?" My colleague replied, "Yes, it happens often".

What followed was a one-on-one between my colleague and the participant,
in the vein of: "But don't you think that happened because of this and
this…" I had stopped following the specifics of the conversation, and was
observing how I had been side-lined from a conversation I had started. I
was also observing how the participants needed to get the white consultant
to offer a 'logical' explanation for an issue I had raised. This example of
people defaulting to a white person, even if I am leading the presentation or
workshop in question, is so common, and shows the strength of the belief
that a white person has more credibility just by being white.

In another incident, together with a white female colleague, I was
interviewing the Board and Exco members of a company in preparation for a
workshop we were planning. It happened about six years ago but I remember
it as clearly as if it was yesterday. During the interview one of the Board

members we were speaking with never once looked at me except when she mentioned something about toilets for disadvantaged people.

To this day I still find that I am sometimes taken more seriously when accompanied by a white consultant, even though I am the Managing Director and owner of my business. These moments reveal people's inner biases and are not limited to race. I also frequently observe the assumption that men know more or are 'in charge'. The examples are endless. If you don't believe me, go to a restaurant and observe how some waiters treat men and women patrons. For our annual year-end function, I always take my staff and colleagues somewhere nice; every year when the bill arrives it is given to a man or a white person. What is so remarkable is how people don't even see that they are doing these things.

My triggers: my inner work

YOU MIGHT THINK that after all these years working in this space I would no longer react to condescending or racist statements. After all, when facilitating workshops, it is my job to hold the group together and take them through the day, so I need to be restrained in responding emotionally to things people say, but the truth is that I am also still triggered from time to time.

Certain words really press my buttons. For example, when someone says, "you people" to refer to black people. Another constant trigger for me is how frequently the words "tokenism" and "black appointment" are used in the same sentence. It is as if you cannot talk about the one without bringing in the other. For example, when you are talking about the need for a company to transform – you need more black executives, more women, etc. – someone will immediately say something like, "We don't want token appointments, we need qualified people". It is as if by talking about transformation I am discounting merit or competence. Meanwhile, when discussing a white candidate, the idea that you would mention the need for "qualified people" is almost unheard of. So when I say "black" and immediately someone talks about "competence", that can really trigger me.

But as I always say to people, what matters is what you *do* with your triggers. Given my line of work, it is essential that I manage my reactions to my triggers. As a facilitator, my role is to create a safe space to hold honest and robust conversations where I can guide people to awareness. If a participant triggers me in a workshop, instead of responding emotionally, I gather my thoughts so I can challenge the participant from a professional space. This means probing the statement by 'holding up the mirror' for the participant to see deeper into themselves through the answers they provide.

For example, if someone said, "Black employees don't stick around because they always respond to the highest bidder", I would ask, "Have you actually taken time to analyse the reasons those particular black people you are referring to have left your organisation? When a white employee leaves for a better opportunity do you make similar comments? Aren't they also responding to the highest bidder?" The best way to lead someone to a position of self-awareness is to use questioning techniques until the person answers their own questions, and through the process hopefully comes to the realisation that they were generalising.

It is through ongoing inner work that I have learned how to manage my feelings and reduce the power that these triggers have on me – but that does not mean I don't feel them. When debates get very heated and my buttons are really pressed, I sometimes use a breathing technique to stay calm, taking three deep breaths and consciously softening my face so it does not betray me. I have gotten feedback that I frown terribly when I am experiencing these things: "Nene, you might be breathing but yoh! Your face!" said one of my colleagues. You have to find a way to deliberately slow down and come across as dignified but firm. In gathering your dignity, you don't want to come across as weak. It's a complex dance of emotions, and it all has to happen in a few seconds.

Another aid is debriefing and peer counselling. Those of us who work in this space sometimes meet together to share coping strategies (for example, one facilitator I know strategically grabs a glass of water when she is triggered). I also have my own ongoing personal coaching process. Having a personal coach or peer coaching sessions where you can share your frustrations and have someone who can 'hold up the mirror' to help you process your own feelings and remind you of the bigger picture as a facilitator is vital to maintaining the joy of facilitation.

Finally, I also am a member of the Diversity Collegium. We are a think-tank of diversity experts and practitioners, and twice a year we meet in a global forum where we share strategies, materials, latest trends, meditations, and support for each other in all kinds of ways. These various support systems are all important to strengthening my resilience and 'staying power' as a diversity and inclusion facilitator.

Undermining your own group

BECAUSE OF THE NATURE OF MY WORK, I often feel I have heard it all when it comes to the ways people exclude or disrespect each other. That said, I still struggle when I come across black people who use racism as an excuse for poor performance. I am constantly fighting this stereotype among white people, so when I see black people doing this, it really throws me off. I want to shout at them, "Don't you know how much extra work you're adding to this?"

I also struggle when in a workshop a black person casually throws insensitive statements and stereotypes at white people, as if because we are so often discriminated against we have a right to do the same to others. Statements like: "You white people have had it nice for so long", "It's our time now" or "Just give way", mostly just get peoples' backs up. There are other better ways of raising the issue of white privilege and the need to level the playing field.

Another complex issue I face is when a black participant challenges me on an example of exclusion that I have highlighted in a workshop. I once related a story of two candidates (one black, one white) who joined a company at the same time as part of the company's internship drive. The white candidate was exposed to more projects and senior people started noticing him, while the black candidate was hardly exposed to similar situations. Obviously, the white candidate progressed faster. After mentioning this, a black workshop participant said, "I have a big problem with black people wanting to be spoon-fed. You must just do your best, and you will be noticed". I kept on explaining that this person was missing the point of the story, but he was adamant that black people want things on a plate and don't want to work hard. I applied the same approach of 'holding up the mirror', asking if he had ever been spoon-fed, but he was getting increasingly irritated and the dynamic threatened to become a dialogue between us, because he clearly was not going to change his perspective. In the end, I had to move on.

These are things I still haven't figured out how to deal with: the so-called black-on-black fight concerning race issues. Am I suggesting that black people cannot challenge each other or challenge me as a facilitator? Not at all. I am simply highlighting the complexity of navigating this journey, and acknowledging that I am still trying to find the most constructive way to handle some of these situations.

ALTHOUGH SO MANY OF THE EXAMPLES I have given here are about race, I face both racism and sexism in my work as a facilitator. When it comes to sexism, what saddens me most is how often sexist remarks in workshops come from women. It is a real example of how internalised oppression can have such power over people.

If you want to create an inclusive culture, sexist jokes should not be tolerated – whether coming from men or women. People will accuse me of making the working environment too rigid, but if people knew how many cases of sexual harassment start with 'little jokes', they might feel differently. I remember one workshop that really pressed my buttons to the limit. I was explaining how leaders must be careful about the language they use – we had been talking about sexist jokes. Two women sitting in a corner said, "Oh come on, you're going overboard. We don't mind those kinds of jokes". They went on and on. I responded by saying that sexist jokes are the same as racist and homophobic jokes, and none of them have a place in an inclusive corporate culture. One of the women wouldn't let it go, trying to draw me into an argument with her. You could see a lot of the men watching this conversation, some now smiling.

I was getting really irritated, but knew I needed to seize control of what was happening. The moment you cross the line and start engaging with participants on their level or come across emotionally, you lose credibility as a facilitator and you lose your audience. One of the men then said very smugly, "You see, where do you draw the line? If women don't know what they want, how should we know?" I had to cut the conversation. I got out of it by saying if they were all okay with that kind of thing in their company then fine for them, but in an inclusive culture it was not okay. Even though my job as a facilitator is to invite all views and really allow people to express themselves fully, I had to change the topic in the interest of keeping control of the workshop.

The thing people often don't realise is that when you are saying these things – racist jokes, homophobic jokes, sexist words – you never know who is around. You might be heterosexual but your son or daughter might be gay or lesbian. If someone tells these jokes in front of you because they think they know you, how are you supposed to feel? They even expect you to laugh with them. Every employee deserves respect and dignity, and you as the person telling a joke need to ask yourself if your joke is really worth putting someone else in an awkward position.

The point is that creating an inclusive environment sometimes means letting certain things go. It's fine for you to attend a comedy show and laugh with your friends at the sexist or racist jokes that comedians tell, but you should really think twice before retelling those jokes at work the next day, especially if you are a leader.

Leaders often like to say they are just "telling it as it is", but the truth is that leaders have an extra responsibility to be aware of the impact of their so-called honesty, especially if that honesty is denigrating certain people. Your positional rank as a leader places an extra burden on you to be careful of what you say. Jokes that denigrate or mock other people often have the double negative effect of elevating your group or subtly communicating your superiority, which is another thing that you as a leader should avoid doing. In the words of Ernest Hemingway, "There is nothing noble in being superior to your fellow men. True nobility lies in being superior to your former self".

The next generation: choosing your battles

This may sound strange given that I grew up in the days of apartheid, but I honestly think that there are new and equally challenging difficulties for young people these days. There is the expectation now that they are in a free society and should be able to fend for themselves, yet the gap between the so-called black middle-class and the critical masses of black people is only widening. Despite the narrative of the B-BBEE enriching black people unfairly, the reality is that less than 1% of JSE-listed companies are owned by black people, and if you go to a township school like Meadowlands High

School where I went, very little has changed in terms of resources. We point to the few middle-class blacks and say things are equal, while forgetting that the critical mass in Soweto, for example, doesn't even know where the private schools are that this small minority attends. Meanwhile, the majority of South African children in rural areas are still going to schools with no proper infrastructure and have to cross dangerous rivers to get there. So how long are we going to tolerate this?

In my day, there was a general understanding that the system was unfair and things were clear. Although no democracy is easy to overhaul, there are areas where we have been lax. We have not implemented many of the things promised, and we need to own up to those failures. Rage and anger are building, and our children are rightly holding us accountable to our promises now.

If I look at what has been going on with the #FeesMustFall' movement[25], I understand why they feel we have let them down. If you go back to the ANC Freedom Charter, it promised free education. The ANC keeps campaigning on free education. So the youth are saying: "We have given you 20 years: where is the education you promised?" People try to backtrack: "No, the Freedom Charter meant x, y, and z", but it clearly said free education for all, so I respect that this generation is demanding that we fulfil our promises. We might not approve of how they have gone about things – I definitely disagree with many of their methods – but I don't see how you can disagree with the mission. The importance of sticking to our promises, being accountable and truthful as leaders – all of this is being shown up.

Meanwhile, people – especially white people – keep saying these kids should be grateful that they are in university in the first place. Again, it is that, 'How dare you demand more?' mentality. There's been so much lack for such a long time, and now when your foot is in, you're supposed to be grateful. But why should our young people be grateful to have a foot in the door? If you are working towards fairness and equality, you can't say you want it in doses only. Either there is equality or there is not.

---

[25] #FeesMustFall is a student-led protest movement that began in October 2015 in response to an increase in fees at South African universities. Although government responded to some of the demands, the issues are far from resolved, and hundreds of millions of Rands of damage have been incurred at universities across South Africa.

My own evolution and learning process tells me that I must not feel guilty to want fairness in my own country, and it is right to want more. But coupled with freedom and fairness are responsibility and accountability. One's personal journey of introspection and self-awareness, standing up for yourself and/or educating others, will always be complex and will challenge you to your very core if you engage in it honestly.

MY OWN CHILDREN are among the black middle-class minority. I see them moving into a new world away from their roots, which worries me sometimes. When my son Motheo was about five years old we were visiting family in Soweto and I had sent him out to play. He came back home early and when I asked why he was back, he told me, "They're speaking in a funny language I can't understand". The "funny language" was isiZulu. I knew on that day I had work to do. I wanted him to be a proud African; to know that he was the same as those kids. When I told him that, he said, "No I'm not". I couldn't blame him: he was still so young and growing up in a totally different environment. But the language my son was using showed me I couldn't leave it at that. Just imagine a so-called diversity and inclusion thought leader's son referring to an African language as "funny". It can be so hard to know what the right thing to do is when navigating all the changes we are living through. The need to help them with speaking English which is a medium of instruction in the world of work and the pride of your African culture and heritage became ever so real for me.

I worry that my kids are losing out on the resilience and strength that come from living in a place like Soweto; from having to make something out of nothing. I also have the right to claim any part of South Africa as my own and have a right to raise my children wherever I choose, but meanwhile I see that they are gaining the knowledge that there is no difference between them and any white person. That is not to say that they couldn't learn that same lesson living in Soweto, but children are masters of observation, and it is naïve to think that living in any of South Africa's townships – where the inequality is so stark – conveys to a child the truth of his equality.

A year ago, I was with my now 16 year old son on a Saturday morning. We were pulling out of the driveway at my house in Norwood, on our way to church. I saw that my roses had blossomed overnight, so I asked him to go inside and bring a pair of scissors and a bowl so I could cut the roses and take them to church. A couple was jogging past as I was cutting the roses and the woman said to the man, "Now you know why you shouldn't plant roses outside your yard – people just take them". I was in complete shock and did nothing for a moment. "You must tell them this is our house!" my Motheo insisted, clearly frustrated. They had not gone far, but I was still working through my own internal anger. Meanwhile, my son was visibly upset, partly because he wouldn't say anything to them himself, thanks to values I have instilled in him that for as long as he was below 21 years of age, he must never get into a slinging match with an adult. It does not matter who is wrong, he must just walk away. I decided to leave it mainly because by the time I could have responded, I would have had to shout for them to hear. I knew it was improbable that they would look back, and my shouting would have probably just confirmed their stereotype of 'angry black women who shout'. Despite the unsatisfying end for my son, I was proud of both his outrage and his restraint.

THIS LEADS ME BACK to a subject I touched on in Chapter 4. When choosing my battles, I sometimes decide that acting contrary to a stereotype is more important than 'standing up' for myself. Transformation fatigue from constantly fighting is very real. On top of the exhaustion you can feel when dealing with these things on a daily basis, the added weight of someone else challenging your response can just be too much, especially when that person is white.

Recently I was in Germany, where I was facilitating a workshop on unconscious bias. I was part of a team with two other South Africans who were both white males. The three of us were supposed to be in Hamburg for a four-day programme and my slot was on the last day. After I had given my lecture, one of my colleagues saw that I was in a hurry to finish and get to the airport. "Why are you leaving so soon? Don't you want to see the city?" he asked. I explained that my visa expired on that very day. "Don't you also have to leave today?" I asked him. After all, we had the same invitation letter to work on the same programme.

It turned out he had been given a visa that was valid for one year. Mine was good only for the four days of the programme. In total disbelief, we checked with our other colleague, also a white male, who also had been given a year. My colleague, who really felt bad, tried to rationalise things and say maybe it's because I had not been to Germany before and he and the colleague had been so their visas were based on that history. I smiled and told him that I had actually been to Munich and Berlin on two separate occasions and we both laughed. All three of us were South African. So I explained to them, "You see, this is what I am talking about – half the things that happen to me you are not even aware of. As a white male you have rank, power, and privilege, your surname probably sounded more 'trustworthy' and without even opening your mouth, you were granted longer days than me. So please trust my decisions. I'd be a lunatic if I fought every little thing". Sometimes it is important to just step back and breathe instead of getting angry and disturbing your inner peace all the time.

In just a second you can oscillate from anger to frustration, disappointment and even laughing at yourself. Sometimes the discussions I have with some of my friends when I go home to Soweto are fascinating. To an outside observer these may be interpreted as downright racist, like when my friend really wanted to know if I genuinely regarded a white person as a friend. They expressed shock that I can spend so much time with white people, asking things like, "Don't they discriminate against you? What do you talk about?", adding a bit of township lingo, "Ahh wena dingamla di feditse ka wena" (whites have won you over and have finished with you – you are totally assimilated to their culture); sometimes I don't even know where to start. Once when I tried to explain that whites are just people, she cut me off, insisting that there is not a single white person who can be fair to a black person. I almost felt like she was accusing me of lying. She spoke with such passion, trying to convince me that I didn't know what was going on. "They've played with your head, my friend, they are not like that, they just want you to see them differently." Sometimes you have to see that you are not going to win a particular battle, but I still find it hurtful to hear things like this. This is a classic case of Intent vs. Impact; whether bias is conscious or unconscious, the impact is the same.

For me, the operative word in all of this is respect. I don't have to agree with you, but I need to treat you as a human being. And when you don't listen – maybe you can't, maybe you don't want to, whatever the reason – you miss out on the possibility of treating another human being with the basic respect we all deserve and crave.

Blind Spots

THROUGH ALL OF MY EXPERIENCES of and with diversity and inclusion, I cannot lie and say that my reality as a black person is not the strongest aspect of my identity as a South African and as someone working with corporates and how I am treated in society. It determined the location and place where I was born: I lived in Soweto because I am black. I went to Meadowlands High School with no maths and science teachers because I am black. My blackness is imprinted on my body and my face; my identity as a black person is only second to my identity as a Child of God. Being black is the lens through which I have always seen life from my upbringing, and the lens through which the world sees and treats me. Even as an owner of a company working in the field of awaking people's consciousness, I am seen through this lens. Even in 2017, race is ever-present, even if it looks different than it used to. I live in a neighbourhood with white neighbours, and my son goes to a school where his closest friends are of Greek, Chinese, Indian and South African origins, but race still segregates us in subtle yet deep ways.

Maybe it is because of my awareness of race and how deeply it still separates us that I struggle to get away from race when I make mistakes. No matter how much I tell myself not to think this way, I immediately worry that if I make a mistake people will say, "It's because it's a black company", never just a simple human error. So that is my ongoing inner work; it is tough and it irritates me, because like everyone, I make mistakes. I have learnt to recognise this toxic narrative – to name it for what it is so that I can isolate it and deal with it appropriately.

Recently I was working with a group of participants and one of them was blind. I had prepared all the materials in braille and sent them ahead of time because I was informed a week before that there would be a blind person in my class, but then we did an exercise that is conducted in complete silence. Explaining the exercise, I said that if during the exercise anyone didn't understand what was going on, "just do this" (and I raised my hand). The other participants looked at me strangely and one of them said, "What do you mean?" Clueless and totally oblivious to my unconscious bias, I raised my hand again, repeating (with a slight of irritation for having to explain myself three times), "Do this". There I was, caught in my own unconsciousness, not even registering what the problem was, until finally one participant moved closer to the one who was blind and said, "I think what Nene is saying is that you must raise your hand". I was utterly embarrassed; I could feel my palms heating up. I always tell my fellow consultants that to recover from a mistake like this, just admit your error and don't try to be smart or to hide it. People are usually very forgiving if your attitude is genuinely apologetic. So that is what I did, and luckily for me the participant in question laughed along with everyone.

Part of learning is accepting that you can make mistakes – very embarrassing mistakes – and owning them immediately after realising or being made aware. The first rule of a good apology is not to get too convoluted. You don't need a three-page explanation; just say sorry and mean it. People usually forgive if your attitude is right. There are always exceptions to this rule of forgiveness, however. In my particular case in that workshop, I was so unsettled that even when the person laughed in what seemed to be 'letting me off the hook', I made it a point that after lunch I spoke to him with the seriousness he deserved, and he accepted my apology.

Recently I was in Minneapolis (USA) facilitating conversations on race. As people entered the room I said that we were going to sit in a circle, and said to the one participant who also happened to have a physical disability, "Don't worry, I'll help you". Immediately a woman who had come to the dialogue said to me, "Excuse me, you haven't even asked 'Do you need my help – you just assume he needs your help?'" I wasn't sure if she knew him or if he agreed with her, but what I did know was that the incident exposed how this was the area of diversity where I had the least experience and needed to do more personal work. I looked to the man for help but he didn't give me any kind of feedback. I didn't know what to do and it really worried me. The schedule was tight and we had to start the session, which ended up being a heated dialogue – nothing to do with the incident – but then we ran out of time. When we finished, people rushed off to the next session and I also had to go and facilitate another group. Throughout the session though, I had been waiting for a chance to speak to him, to ask if he had been offended and to find out what I should have said. But I never got a chance, so I never got closure. The best I could do as a gift to myself was to do inner work about this aspect of diversity. It is still a work in progress, but once you admit that something is challenging you and you commit to doing something about it and look for a social partner, then you are well on your way to personal development and growth. It is work in progress and the operative word there is 'progress'.

Towards the future

IF I HAD TO CHOOSE ONE THING for everyone to do to help us move towards the larger culture change we need in this country, it would be for more people to just ask people who are different to tell them their stories. Ask someone to tell you her story and do not edit it. For example, if I ask a girl who is now at Meadowlands High School to tell me her story, I need to listen without interjecting my perception of how it was when I was there. If you take over a person's story and tell it, or start a story from 'secondly', you come out with a totally different story. Everyone has her own story, from her own worldview, and her own unique experience. Once I start adding my memories or perceptions of Meadowlands I begin punctuating her story, telling her where to end it, where it should be painful, what the punch line should be, and then I am stealing her story. The art of listening is hearing what is emerging from what someone is saying, so that in my understanding we can build something new. This is the first point of respect – hear someone's story.

The second thing, especially for leaders, is to recognise that no one can ever teach you nuances. A nuance is just that. There are things that will be difficult to pick up just by the nature of who you are, so when we talk diversity and inclusion, there are certain things that cannot be explained by a logical 1 + 1 = 2, especially when it comes to issues of discrimination. I often hear leaders say, "Tell me exactly what the person did. Give me hard facts, then I will tell you whether you are right to feel the way you are feeling". Rather say, "How did it make you feel when that person said that?" The way you ask a question acknowledges nuance and allows or prevents it from emerging in a conversation. In the end, the subtleties of discrimination usually reside in nuance.

The need to debrief and get a coach as a facilitator

Facilitators also need coaches and people to bounce ideas off or a go-to person to deepen your own learning. My coach, friend and sounding board for the past 12 years has been Heidi Carter. We met for the first time when I went to facilitate a diversity game at a school in Johannesburg and we just clicked. She later became my coach. The relationship advanced to later becoming friends. I have learnt so much from Heidi because of her seasoned consulting and coaching background. I never understood why someone who did work somewhat similar to mine would be willing to be a sounding board without hesitation. Yes, she was my coach but she also did work on culture change. If you want to see someone with the spirit of giving and abundance, I would point you to Heidi.

I do also play a role as her sounding board. Whenever both of us have had a 'difficult' session with a client, we call each other and just ventilate and reflect together in supportive way. I also give her feedback that if you say XYZ, you come across in this way and this is the impact that it has on me as a black person. We all need such friends and people in our professional lives. She always says, "Nene, please protect me with the truth", and I believe that this is critical for authentic relationships. Get a buddy to serve as your mirror for your own inner work on transformation. Everyone needs a 'heart keeper' in life – someone you'd not hesitate to pick up a phone and open your heart to, to share even the most embarrassing professional 'oops' moments and ask for guidance. Another friend who has played that pivotal role in my life is Merafe Ramono. A friendship that spans over three decades from when we were at UCT right through my working life, Merafe is that kind of a friend who is values-driven and offers solid advice that will bring me back to a moral compass that resonates with me. In addition, he is my 'go to' person to construct a good English expression or concept, who would interpret complex scenarios and simplify them to ensure good dialogue in my facilitation sessions. On the many times I felt like quitting, he would simply say, "I don't know why you get so worked up, no one said transformation was easy – you are definitely doing something right".

Finally, this journey of transformation is hard and humbling and will expose to you your own vulnerabilities and things that might be unpleasant to acknowledge. But never give up, never take anything you have for granted, and never forget that you are where you are because others decided to give of themselves. As Warren Buffett once said, "Someone is sitting in the shade today because someone planted a tree a long time ago". No matter who you are, you have a responsibility to uplift and be present for others where you can. Every one of us has a role to play in breaking down our differences to find our similarities and a shared path to a more inclusive, dynamic, innovative, creative, and yes, better, world.

INSIGHTS & TIPS

Even as someone who has worked for years in the field of transformation, diversity and inclusion, I still have to do my own inner work, managing my triggers and authentically apologising when I make a mistake. This work is ongoing for all of us and can ultimately lead to a world where we can all feel a sense of belonging.

Inner work is never 'done'

Recognise and work with your triggers

 Practical Tips

- Keep analysing and looking at how you speak, act, etc.

- Listen to the feedback people give you in an open and receptive way and be willing to change if needed.

- Have trustworthy support groups that provide:

  o peer counselling; and

  o a space to debrief when your triggers are pushed.

- Engage in ongoing personal coaching if possible.

Stop undermining the transformation of your own group(s)

Work for greater understanding across all groups

 Practical Tips

- Be aware of the power of internalised oppression. When Steve Biko said, "The most potent weapon in the hands of the oppressor is the mind of the oppressed", this is significant because once you have believed the story that you are 'less than', then the cycle of inferiority is self-perpetuating. Do inner work and unlearn the negative stories you were taught about yourself.

- Challenge yourself and unzip your own baggage to empty it of self-denigrating messages about people of your gender or race group.

- Accept that subliminal messages have been embedded throughout decades, and just because you hear a story repeated does not mean that it is true.

Challenge inappropriate jokes

Build an inclusive environment through awareness of your choice of words and comments

 Practical Tips

- Be conscious of who is in hearing of your 'jokes' and comments.

- If you are from the dominant culture you need to be particularly careful of telling jokes about minority groups.

- If members of a minority group tell self-denigrating jokes about themselves or their group, it is still not ok.

- As a leader, it is your impact not your intention that matters.

We all make mistakes: learn to apologise

Be conscious of how you apologise when you make a mistake

Practical Tips

- Once you have offended someone, don't minimise their feelings by referring to your intention. Instead, own up to the impact of your behaviour. It is so important to know how and when to apologise. The general principle is that the best apology is changed behaviour because repeat behaviour with constant apology renders it meaningless. In the meantime:

  ○ Take responsibility: understand impact versus intent. Express regret and show remorse, be brief and to the point.

  ○ Avoid using conditional language like 'if's' and 'but's'.

  ○ Never find comfort in thinking: "Well, I'm not the only one who feels this way."

  ○ Make amends. If there is anything you can do to mend the situation, do it.

  ○ Do your best and let go of the outcome of your apology. It may or may not be accepted and you cannot control the other person's response. Let it go.

  ○ To the recipients of the apology, try to accept it and do not lump everyone together who looks like the offender.

Don't give up the fight

Working at transformation, despite the challenges, will pay off

 ## Practical Tips

- Never forget all the people who helped you get where you are.

- Remember that giving of yourself is how you will leave a legacy and contribute to building the next generation of leaders.

Index

CPSIA information can be obtained
at www.ICGtesting.com
Printed in the USA
LVHW080212250719
625290LV00007B/34/P